THE QUIET VOICE OF SOUL

How to Find Meaning in Ordinary Life

Tian Dayton, Ph.D.

Health Communications, Inc.
Deerfield Beach, Florida

Library of Congress Cataloging-in-Publication Data

Dayton, Tian.
  The quiet voice of soul: how to find meaning in ordinary
life/Tian Dayton.
  p. cm.
    ISBN 1-55874-339-1 (pbk.)
    1. Spiritual life. 2. Soul. I. Title.
BL624.D36 1995
158--dc20   95-11849
                                                            CIP

©1995 Tian Dayton
ISBN 1-55874-339-1

Publisher: Health Communications, Inc.
              3201 S.W. 15th Street
              Deerfield Beach, Florida 33442-8190
Cover design by Andrea Perrine Brower
Cover photo by A & V Downes

To Mom and Walt
with love

CONTENTS

6. HEALING THE WOUNDED SELF

7. HIDING FROM THE SELF

8. PASSAGES

9. BALANCE

10. PLAY

11. UNIVERSE

12. SPIRITUALITY

INTRODUCTION

THE QUIET VOICE OF SOUL

*When an ordinary man attains knowledge he is
a sage; when a sage attains understanding, he is
an ordinary man.*

Zen saying

The afternoon was quiet. Across the lawn, leaves rus-
tled softly in a breeze that passed in all directions. The
rolling hills created a soft horizon that seemed to go on
and on in a gentle motion across everything that could be
seen. The heat of the day hung in the air, slowly giving
way to the cooler air beneath it. The tea had the slightest
bite to it, and the atmosphere felt as if it were softly fold-
ing in on itself. One deep, long and beautiful moment, a
summer afternoon. The soul that lay beneath this moment

was like heat rising from a hot brick, filled with tranquility, splendor and gentleness, the quiet subtle connection
with the eternal. Time was standing still. Here it is, I
thought. I am surrounded by it. It is enough.

❧

All too often we consider that the soul is something we
have to strive for, to run toward, bettering ourselves until
that moment when we are good enough finally to be with
it. We think we must live the right life, thinking just the
right thoughts, so that one day we will get lucky—somehow the trap door will fly open and we will see our souls.
In this endless pursuit of soul, we miss it altogether
because soul is present at all times in all things. The soul's
energy resides in all that is living, including ourselves. The
soul is a constant; it is we who waver from it. That is why
the path to self is also the path to soul. We do not need to
search the world over until we finally find it; we need only
to look in ourselves, to be willing to journey into our own
depths. When we are willing to experience all of it—the
good and the bad, the beautiful and the ugly, to be with
all that we are—we will experience an illumination that
reveals the soul to be right where it always was: within us.

❧

Plotinus speaks of the individual soul as indivisible
from the All Soul. That is, each of us has encoded into our
physical, emotional and spiritual being the same stuff of
soul contained in the very heart of God. In fact, we are
that heart or that soul, if you will, one and the same. There
is no moment in life when we are separate from soul, no
place to go that is without the presence of soul. Soul is

anywhere and everywhere. As we deepen our ability to sit quietly within ourselves, to be present in the here and now, we deepen our connection with our own individual soul which is connected to, and made of the same stuff as, the universal soul.

Said another way, your individual soul is that energy that vivifies or animates your body and mind, and it is unique to you. It is as intrinsic and necessary to your life as your breath, and as intimately yours as the cells in your bone marrow. Each individual soul has a quality that has been called the God Seed, because it participates in, is part of, the universal energy called God. Soul, then, is both personal and universal, intimate, infinite, inescapable and the absolutely most authentic element of each individual. It is that part of us that lives life and transcends life.

While our souls transcend the Earth, our bodies are dependent on the Earth for continuing life. It's vital that, in our effort to deepen our soul life, we don't begin to disdain our Earthly, earthy connection. Both are essential. Both are divine. Ordinary souls live ordinary lives with eternal significance.

Soul seems mysterious because we cannot see it. Often we seek knowledge and experience of the soul in the extraordinary. But I believe that soul is fundamentally *ordinary*, available to us all the time. If it is not present in the act of tidying a room or walking a child to school, then it cannot be present anywhere else. We do not have to feel pressured to select the correct activity by which to know the soul because the soul is everywhere, and the correct activity is always at hand, constantly presenting itself. You are engaging in it right now.

Getting to know the soul takes a simple shift in awareness. We do not have to look outside ourselves to find soul;

we only have to remove the emotional, psychological and intellectual blocks that we put in the way of our soul's expression. In this book we will look at the kinds of thinking and behavior that prevent us from experiencing soul energy in day-to-day living. We will learn how to see the soul's presence, not only in the mysteries of the universe, but in the more familiar daily wonders of ordinary life.

Though soul is mysterious, it is hardly inaccessible. It is with us all the time, waiting to be discovered. In my work as a therapist involved with psychodrama and role enactment, I have seen the truths of the soul expressed over and over again in infinite and wonderful variety. The soul is always there. It's up to us to make contact.

Life is the laboratory of soul growth; the daily situations and circumstances that we encounter are the means through which we investigate our very selves, grist for the mill of soulmaking. When we learn to use everyday life as our personal journey toward self and soul, we grow gradually toward a higher state of consciousness and a more meaningful existence.

The sections at the end of each chapter called Bonding with the Soul are there for you. They are opportunities for you to use the physical and psychological situations in your life as vehicles for soul growth. It was John Keats who said, "call the world, if you please, the vale of soulmaking." Use the exercises, then, as your personal journal of soulmaking, your path toward your own individual soul.

Use this book as you might use a diary or journal. Interact with it, write in the margins; let it happen to you, with you and for you. Make it your own. The exercises at the end of each chapter are there for you. Play with them, adjust them to suit you—work with them in whatever way works best for you.

This book is a journey of soul discovery. In its pages you will find that the soul calls to us in many ways—through our families, our relationships, our feelings; through play, through the universe and, of course, through spirituality. I wish you a pleasant journey.

1
Self

ANSWERING THE CALL OF THE SELF

*How shall I grasp it? Do not grasp it. That
which remains when there is no more grasping is the self.*

Panchadari

When our son was in third grade, I asked him why he didn't
want to sign up for after-school activities. His eyes deepened. He
stood up and looked out the window, and I could see he was tun-
ing in on himself before he replied. "To be honest, Mom, I don't
have time."

*The most terrify-
ing thing is to
accept oneself
completely.*

Carl Jung

When I asked him what he meant by that, he
explained. "I need to come home and have time to
play, to watch cartoons, to be with you, to play
with all the toys in my room, sometimes just to
walk around my room, maybe go to the store and
have time to play with my friends in the building." He said that all
day people told him what to do, and there was no way he was going
to put himself in a situation where people were going to continue to
tell him what to do after school.

To me this reflected a simple and direct understanding of what
made him happy and rounded out his life to his satisfaction. He
understood the joy and the serenity that simple things brought to him.
He seemed wholly unfettered by the thought that he might be missing out on something or that he was not doing what his good friends
at school were doing. He was not anxious that he was not following
their program because he was in touch with what felt good to him.

I have always enjoyed my son's company because he is so present in the moment. Being with him can make the most ordinary
activity seem fun and exciting. To be in tune with the moment is to
be in tune with life's subtle pulse and to have at your fingertips the
wisdom of saints and sages. Ultimately, becoming more spiritual will

not make life something different. What will change is how we experience the life we have.

❧

Instead of standing on the shore and proving to ourselves that the ocean cannot carry us, let us venture on its waters just to see.

Pierre Teilhard de Chardin

SOUL AND SELF

We have now discovered that it was an intellectually unjustified presumption on our forefathers' part to assume that Man has a Soul; . . . that there is a power inherent in it which builds up the body, supports its life, heals its ills and enables the soul to live independently of the body; . . . and that beyond our empirical present, there is a spiritual world from which the soul receives knowledge of spiritual things whose origins cannot be discovered in this physical world. But . . . it is just as presumptuous and fantastic for us to assume that matter produces spirit; that apes give rise to human beings; . . . that the brain cells manufacture thoughts and that all this could not possibly be other than it is.

Carl Jung

The individual self is the channel through which the soul finds expression. If it is tangled in the ropes of self-hatred, false identity and confusion, the soul will have a difficult time shining through. When life is confusing or overwhelming, or when our lives allow little room for personalized variation—in a troubled family or an autocratic workplace, for example—the self goes into hiding. When this happens, we learn to look outward rather than inward for answers.

Often soul is not regarded as a part of ordinary life, but as something belonging to the sphere of religion or metaphysics. But individually we have the right to open communication with soul, just as we have the right to feel the sun on our face and to breathe the air that surrounds us. Access to soul energy enhances access to *ourselves*, and to a deeper reality. Although we cannot necessarily describe this other reality, we can experience and share it with others who also are able to experience it.

Many people who seek an inward path go into therapy to begin to untie their personal knots and solve emotional issues. Most paths to self have two or more people to anchor the experience or create a holding environment, whether it is the relationship between guru and disciple, therapist and client, sponsor and sponsored, pastor and parishioner, teacher and student, or individual and group. It appears that we need a guide to show the way and to help anchor the way as we seek ourselves, someone who is willing to walk with us as we keep ourselves on our path. As C. S. Lewis said, "It takes two to see one."

In my work as a psychodramatist, *I* do not heal my clients. Rather, I involve people in the process of accessing their *own* internal healer. A trusting relationship with a teacher or guide is important to "hold" our growth process, but the ultimate responsibility remains with the self. Therapy is both a process of dismantling and reexamining problem aspects of the self and rebuilding and reshaping from the inside out. Healing and soul growth are part of the mystery of life.

Therapy is a step on the way to soul realization, not an end in itself. If we spin forever in the cycle of sorting out the past without continuing the movement toward soul and self, we may become victimized by our own search. The goal of therapy is to make the unconscious conscious, to bring psychological and behavioral patterns and repetitions into the light. Then we can see the patterns for what they are, understand their cause, release them and reintegrate them back into our unconscious in a resolved state.

Though thou hast ever so many counselors, yet do not forsake the counsel of your own soul.

John Ray

In the process we achieve a less contaminated vision of who we are, and of that part of ourselves that is alive and connected to spirit.

In this light, we can see that the self and the soul are truly a source of nurturance that is always available. When we do not see the soul as this, we deny ourselves a fundamental source of sustenance. When we see the soul as something we have to attain or run after, we diminish it in depth and breadth and throw it outside the self onto the pile of objects that we must acquire. The soul can never be acquired by running after it. Only by sitting in stillness with it can we come to know it.

The path to soul is a path of gradual involvement. It is a process of getting to know the soul and self through direct experience. The reason a therapeutic process is so helpful on the road to self is that, when we sit quietly with ourselves, all of the unfinished business, the old hurts and unquenched longings, begin to rumble around and make themselves felt. If we cannot remain present through this process of feeling our painful feelings, sorting through them and resolving them, we cannot remain present with ourselves. When we have sorted out the problem and learned methods of being with our inner pain rather than running from it, we can *sit* through these feelings and eventually get to serenity with self, and through that, to soul.

All too often the therapeutic process is regarded as an end in itself when actually it is a path, a process to connect us with our soul. Some use therapy as a means to build spiritual consciousness. If we seek only spiritual consciousness and refuse to work through our own darkest depths, what we pursue is *God thinking* or the practice of thinking spiritual thoughts because we have read or heard them and recognize their benefit. We need to go deeper to contact our spirit, the soul that lives within us, that soul we can contact through quiet and meditation. Once we have learned to access the soul through stillness, we can then draw this consciousness actively through ourselves and into our lives.

My greatest teachers are the afflicted. Go to them in jails, in hospitals, and ask, "Why do you want to live?" I walked through hospital corridors, going into rooms, asking people who had things I was afraid of, "Why do you want to live? How do you manage?" They were always honest and willing to help. Some said, "Sit down, I'll tell you." Others said, "Come back, I'll make a list for you." What impressed me was that the list did not contain pages of philosophical discussion about the meaning of life. They said things that were so simple. "I painted a picture," said someone with no fingers: a brush had to be tied to her hand. "I looked out the window, and it is a beautiful day." "The nurse rubbed my back." "My family called and are coming to see me." The lists just went on with simple daily events. And I began to realize that this is really what life is about.

Bernie S. Siegel, M.D.

THE SHADOW SELF

*Knowing your own darkness is the best method
for dealing with the darkness of other people.*

Carl Jung

When there are parts of ourselves that we feel are not acceptable, either to ourselves or to our world, we cast them into a darkness deep in our psyches. These parts of ourselves coalesce to form what Carl Jung called the "shadow self," or the self whose existence we attempt to deny. Although we deny this self consciously, unconsciously we fear that we carry within us something monstrous that threatens to rear its head if we do not use our psychic energy to keep it hidden.

Inevitably, however, that monster refuses to stay hidden. What we refuse to see or acknowledge in ourselves, we identify readily in others. Often we are projecting our unwanted characteristic onto another person, attributing it only to them rather than accepting it as part of ourselves. It is an unconscious attempt to give voice and shape to that part of ourselves we have silenced. When we have a powerful reaction to a characteristic that we classify as negative or difficult in another person, it is worthwhile to ask ourselves if any part of that characteristic exists in us.

Those parts of ourselves that we feel are well hidden are only too evident to those around us. When we hold parts of ourselves in dark-

A person who is always nice is not always nice.

Polish proverb

ness, refusing to own them in the light of day, they are still present in the emotional environment we create. Then the classic double message results. People close to us feel one thing, perhaps anger, but see and hear another, perhaps our message of sweet accommodation. When the messages we send feel mixed to those around us, they become confused and find it hard to locate and relate to us for any substantial length of time.

Clearly, the parts of ourselves that we refuse to bring into con-sciousness speak loudly nonetheless. A way to resolve this dilemma is to bring them to consciousness and allow them voice. When they are brought to consciousness, owned and shared, they lose their inner grip. They no longer need to be acted out because now they can be talked out.

"Yea, though I walk through the valley of the shadow of death" can be understood as the walk through our own dark side. Without the understanding gained in such a walk, we cannot be fully present with our own inner selves, our path to our individual souls.

Acknowledging and working with our own dark side is vital to soul growth and self-awareness. Conducting our lives as if we do not have a dark side forces significant parts of the self into hiding and cre-ates a fake, unstable personality in which we con-stantly have to pretend those aspects don't exist. We weaken our position by not accepting fully where we

A horse may run quickly, but it cannot escape its own tail.

Russian proverb

are and we send a negative message to the self, telling it to hide in shame. This hiding gives negative feelings power. They build frustration and come out in rash, irrational, often destructive ways. Disowned aspects of the self can become dangerous if they are not accepted, worked through and integrated.

The alternative is not in seeking to be perfect. We need not be perfect to be good, productive, healthy people. In fact, that very drive toward perfection can create and strengthen the shadow self. What we seek is balance between our inner and outer expressions of self.

The soul and the self, in order to be experienced, need to be known. Disowned aspects of the self literally cast a shadow over the soul that keeps it from being seen and felt.

❦

If only there were evil people somewhere, insidiously committing evil deeds, and it were necessary only to separate them from the rest of us and destroy them. But the line dividing good and evil cuts through the heart of every human being. And who is willing to destroy a piece of his own heart?

Alexander Solzhenitsyn

GETTING TO KNOW YOURSELF

The mind is its own place, and in itself, can make a Heaven of Hell, a Hell of Heaven.

John Milton

Most people come into therapy in an attempt to rid their personalities of what they perceive to be undesirable aspects. But in the process, rather than get rid of parts of themselves, they learn to work with the troublesome areas and reintegrate them in a new way. In fact, getting to know ourselves is one of the more rewarding and powerful adventures we can have. It is a lifelong task because the

Being entirely honest with oneself is a good exercise.

Sigmund Freud

self is in continual evolution. The more comfortable we are with ourselves, the easier it will be to get out of our own way and allow the deeper pulse of life and love and spiritual energy to flow through us.

Sometimes we see the therapeutic process as a sort of psychic diet in which we come in overweight and leave slimmer, with less psychic baggage. Ultimately, any responsible therapeutic process leads us toward ourselves rather than away, and helps us to get our personalities in clear enough perspective that they do not overwhelm our souls with unmet needs and unquenchable desires.

The therapeutic process can also help us get in touch with our natural healing forces. Tapping into these forces and working with them to relieve the psychic system of toxicity, pain and undesirable self-concepts is part of healing. When the emotional pain is purged or released, we are free to see things differently and can examine ourselves more openly.

Inner growth involves a shift in perception. Carl Jung said that we never really solve a problem; we simply go to the top of a mountain, or a high place within ourselves, and learn to see the situation differently. These shifts in perception create shifts in self-concept and shifts in the way we live our lives. In getting to know ourselves we are not going on an archeological dig for a hidden self, but learning to see evidence of the self in all things. We are allowing the self to emerge, not battling it to remain hidden, and inviting the self to come forward in a self-accepting, self-caring way so that we can better know it.

We can take this caring position with ourselves, creating an inner climate of love and acceptance in which we would no more squash the self because we find it undesirable than we would squash the child who is innocent and filled with life and excited to share her discoveries, her joy and pain, her excitement and despair.

To be loving to the self is a much more demanding task than being in love with the self. To this end, you might treat your emerging self the way a grandparent would. A grandparent has lived long enough and has enough separation from the grandchild to understand the value of indulgence and to allow the child a wide berth for self-explo-

A miracle is a shift in perception.

Course In Miracles

ration, while still being a compassionate and safe point of reference, grounding and boundary setting. When the self has to prove itself to be acceptable to us, we will never live without anxiety. In order to be fully experienced, the self needs just to be at rest in our compassion and love.

❧

Know then thyself, presume not God to scan:
The proper study of mankind is man.

Alexander Pope

FALSE IDENTIFICATION

Every real object must cease to be what it
seemed, and nor could ever be what the whole soul desired.

George Santayana

Christianity teaches that the spirit of God is within us. Vedanta philosophy holds that there is only one true identification: with the eternal self that is present in each of us. Any other identification, with things outside of ourselves, is a false identification. Placing meaning where meaning is not and cannot be generated causes us to move away from our own soul.

Unfortunately, false identification is what we do much of the time. For instance, while Morgan was shopping, a careless driver rammed his car. Angry and hurt, he complained to his friend Sarah, "I got a dent!" For a moment, Sarah stared at him with some bewilderment, since Morgan didn't look dented visibly. Belatedly, she realized that Morgan was referring not to himself, but to his car. Morgan's identification with his car was so strong that when his car got dented, he reported that *he* was dented.

Of course, this can be simply a way of speaking, but it can also reflect a deep identification with the things we own. When we identify falsely with people, places and things outside of ourselves, we lose a piece of our soul to them. When we allow the objects in our lives to carry more meaning than we carry within ourselves, we feel diminished and smaller than everything that surrounds us. We engage in a child-like relationship to the people, places and things that we have accumulated. We assign them authority and we indenture ourselves to that authority.

There is nothing everlasting about a table or a painting or a car, but the human spirit is eternal. That link with eternity is available to us at all times, waiting for us to tap into it.

❧

Attachment is the great fabricator of illusions;
reality can be attained only by someone who is detached.

Simone Weil

LEARNING

What one knows is, in youth, of little moment;
they know enough who know how to learn.

Henry Adams

How many times have you gone grocery shopping and witnessed a scene like this? A parent is pushing a shopping cart through the fruit section, with a two-year-old in the child's seat. The parent picks up some grapefruit, absent-mindedly says, "Grapefruit," and puts them into the cart. The child shrieks, points and says, "Grapefruit!"

Parent:	Grapefruit.
Child:	GRAPEFRUIT!
Parent:	Grapefruit.
Child:	GRAPEFRUIT!
Parent:	Yes, grapefruit . . .
Child:	Daddy, GRAPEFRUIT!
Parent:	Okay, I said it, grapefruit; you told me ten times!

Has the two-year-old discovered a foolproof way to drive her father nuts? Is this some new form of parent torture? Is she building up to a temper tantrum? No, the two-year-old is building language skills. She has made a connection between the abstract word-symbol "grapefruit" and the physical object. She is repeating it over and over again to anchor the concept on a cognitive level. In short, she is learning.

Learning is a process of paring down and building up brain cells. Learning is stored in cell assemblies. When we take in new information, we weed out what we see as no longer relevant and add what is, forming a new cell assembly. This is how we grow and expand our level of consciousness. It is how we integrate our understanding of any situation, concrete or abstract, including our understanding of soul and self. Our new awareness is added to the appropriate cell assembly to expand and enrich it, while cells storing irrelevant information are weeded out. Then we practice. We repeat what we have learned to anchor the learning, the new thinking or the changed behavior on a cognitive level.

Contrary to what we once thought, the brain may be designed to grow and change throughout our lives. Studies done with a group of nuns in Mankato, Minnesota, demonstrate that the mental diseases of aging can be warded off by continually learning new information or performing exercises that stretch the brain, such as math or crossword puzzles.

We can surmise from this that devoting ourselves to lifelong learning, expansion of consciousness and a continual search to understand the self and soul more fully actually creates health and allows us to live a more meaningful and enjoyable life well into later years. The trick is to continue learning new information and to look at the world around us with a fresh eye. Looking not just to reinforce what we already know, but *to be open to new learning.* This openness keeps both the self and the brain alive and growing.

I have noticed that people with strong spiritual beliefs seem to develop a sort of luminescence in their faces in their later years. Eric Erickson refers to the developmental task of this stage of life as generativity vs. despair. That is, one can either generate personal and spiritual growth or fall into despair. This can also be seen as a new stage of learning, a reviewing of a life's worth of accumulated experience and wisdom along with an incorporation of new spiritual awareness, challenging both the brain and the heart to expand into and live with deeper levels of soul.

✿

If you wish to learn the highest truths, begin with the alphabet.

Japanese proverb

BEING REAL

There is no reality except the one contained within us. This is why so many people lead such an unreal life. They take the images outside them for reality and never allow the world within to assert itself.

Herman Hesse

Being real implies that we can be with ourselves, that we know what is going on inside of us. We know when we meet someone we like, when we meet someone we don't like, and we have some sense of why. We know which activities bring us pleasure, and what work undertakings feel fulfilling because they reflect the values and ambitions that are important to us. We know what foods we like to eat, what clothes we are comfortable in and what kind of lifestyle might best suit us. We know how we prefer to spend our weekends, what kind of socializing is our kind of socializing. Most important of all, from hour to hour during the course of any given day, if asked how we were, we would be able to reply.

> *I will work in my own way, according to the light that is in me.*
>
> Lydia Maria Child

This kind of being real enables us to meet life's complications with some semblance of security that we will survive them, and with some deeper understanding that we will probably come out better for having done so.

On the other hand, there is the phony act some people have learned of miming sincerity. Madison Avenue has used "real" to sell everything from aspirin to yogurt. We have all been with people who have a good "real" act: They make deep eye contact, and then they "share" more intimate details than are appropriate to the situation. This false sincerity has a rehearsed quality; it lacks spontaneity, true connection and knowledge of the self. Being real implies that the silver threads of consciousness are connected inwardly, from emotion to thought to cognition to fantasy. Impulses, yearnings and dreams have a central meeting place, and there we can call on them to release information about the self.

Truly being real asks us to be willing to be in touch with our self even when what comes up is not exactly what our vanity might wish for. It asks us to understand that we are in a continual state of becoming. To be real we must content ourselves with the thought that we will never be completely within our own view. Rather, we will catch glimpses of what is going on for us at a particular moment. In order to be real, we must give our self room to express itself naturally and fluidly according to what it is, not according to the dictates of what we perceive to be most palatable to our idealized image of ourselves.

Be yourself, that's all there is of you.

Emerson

The energy of soul does not disappear when we are not aware of it. It does not disappear when we are pretending to be real. It just waits for us to discover it, to be willing to allow it to breathe through us and enable it to be present.

❦

If it were possible to talk to the unborn, one could never explain to them how it feels to be alive, for life is washed in the speechless real.

Jacques Barzun

BONDING WITH THE SOUL

MOMENT OF EMPOWERMENT

Reflection: Choose a time in your life when you felt particularly proud or good about yourself. It may be a period in your life or a single event. Allow yourself to come onto the stage of your mind. How did you look at the time you have chosen? Picture yourself. What are you wearing? How do you stand? What is the expression on your face and in your eyes? Now mentally reverse roles and become yourself at that period in your life; become the image in your mind.

Journal: Now that you have reversed roles with yourself at that period in your life, write a monologue describing yourself and expressing all of who you are at that stage. For example, "I am 8 years old, my name is Marina and I think I am beautiful. Recently, I was the star in my school play. Everyone thought I did a wonderful job and I felt that I was a star, capable and talented."

Continue to write in this fashion until you have said everything that you want to say, then reverse roles again. How can you enjoy this part of yourself in your life today?

BONDING WITH THE SOUL

MEETING MYSELF

Reflection: Think of an age that was significant in some way for you. When you have the age in mind, imagine yourself and the world that surrounded you at that time. What is it about this time period that feels significant or important? Is there some part of yourself at this time that you wish to understand better or feel connected to? If so, what is it?

Journal: Write journal entries of two characters. One, yourself at that period in your life and the other, yourself today. Write a dialogue that goes back and forth. Use a nickname or whatever name you went by at that time.

After you have finished your vignette, ask yourself what part of this self is still with you today that gives you pleasure. What part of that self is still with you that you can let go of? What are the last things, for now, that you want to say to your self of that time?

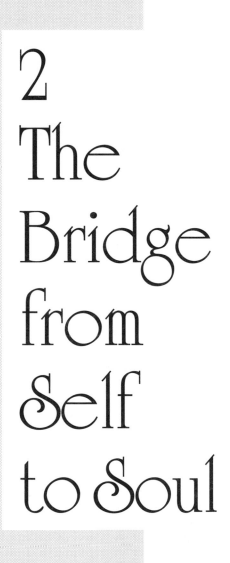

2
The
Bridge
from
Self
to Soul

SEEING THE SOUL AS SEPARATE

What stuff is the soul made of? The question is as meaningless as asking what stuff citizenship or Wednesdays are made of. The soul is a holistic concept. It is not made of stuff at all. Where is the soul located? Nowhere. To talk of the soul as being in a place is as misconceived as trying to locate the number seven or Beethoven's Fifth Symphony. Such concepts are not in space at all.

Paul Davies, physicist

As long as we see ourselves as separate from our souls, we will be tempted to believe that we can pick soul up and put it on like an old coat. Then when it feels too demanding, too pressing, too urgent, we will feel that we can take it off again, hang it on a hook and ignore it. Seeing the soul as separate from ourselves encourages us to be irresponsible about our own spirituality. If it is separate, we thank it, blame it or forget about it altogether and go about our business without the awareness that living outside of the presence of soul and God is a choice rather than an inevitability.

We are always present simultaneously *to* and *with* soul. To define soul as separate from us is, in a sense, to cast it away, to divide ourselves from our God-based natures. When we cast our souls away from us, where do they go? If soul is everywhere, being separate from it is not possible; so soul identification is not a search, but a recognition. We do not need to search for soul because we are already made of it. What we need to do is to remove those psychological, emotional and spiritual issues and tangles that keep us from being present in the moment, that is, present with soul. Soul is woven into the moment, into the here and now, because the here and now is all that really exists. Every preoccupation we follow that is not based in the here and now is a psychological or emotional departure from the moment, a preoccupation with something outside of the here and now. Though preoccupations are a natural part of daily living, getting lost in them means living our preoccupations as our life. Resolving preoccupations, compulsions and issues from the past that contaminate the present, frees us to be present in the here and now.

The native people who had lived for centuries in the Black Hills of what is now South Dakota understood this quite well. The Black Hills were considered a spiritual place by many people, but when the Europeans settled the area, they built churches and wanted the Native Americans to attend services. Each week, one of the Native Americans walked quietly into the hills with his burro as he did his work. And each week, a particular settler reminded him that he did not come to church to seek God. Each week the Native American listened to him politely, but was confused by what he meant. One week, when the European again asked this man why he neglected to visit God, the man had a sudden insight as to what the question meant.

"I see now," he replied. "Your God lives in a house. You go there to see Him. That's nice. I understand. For me it is different. My God lives everywhere, even in these hills, and is with me all the time."

❧

There is an everywhere unity that applies both to soul itself and its various functions. To identify the relationship of all-SOUL to particular souls, the relationships between a soul and its sensations would entail that no particular soul, but only the all-SOUL could have thought or knowledge; to localize thought is to recognize the separate existence of the individual soul. But since the soul is a rational soul, by the very same title by which it is an all-SOUL, and is called the rational soul, in the sense of being a whole (and so not merely "reasoning locally"), then what is thought of as a part must in reality be no part but the identity of an unparted thing.

Plotinus

THE SPLIT BETWEEN PSYCHOLOGY AND SOUL

Observers are not detached from reality. In the new way of looking at it, the new physics, the observer and the observed are tangled together in an inextricable way. . . . everything is folded together into a unity . . . we really do seem to play a fundamental role in the working of nature, and this I find tremendously inspiring because it seems that my own individual life has more purpose. . . . It's actually interwoven into the nature of reality in a very fundamental way. So in some sense we're not just a trivial add-on into the universe, not like extras that have stumbled onto the great cosmic set just by accident. We're truly written into the script, we're truly meant to be here.

Paul Davies, "The Soul of the Universe"

Although *psyche*, the root of the word psychology, means "soul," the *Encyclopedia of Psychology* has no entry for soul. Our society has somehow come to view the soul as something that does not exist synonymously with mind. But if the soul is not simultaneously present with the mind, then where is it? If soul is not a part of our concept of psychology, then how do we connect our intellectual, emotional and spiritual selves?

When we separate the body, mind and spirit, we do not allow our full being to work as it was meant to, as an integrated whole. We leave significant parts of ourselves out, relegating and managing them or asking them to disappear altogether. This makes as little sense as eating without tasting. When we separate the soul and the mind, we put ourselves at a similar disadvantage.

Psychology was informed by the Newtonian model of science, which encouraged us to think of everything as separate, including ourselves. Quantum physics refutes that by giving us a new model in which we are not separate entities, but overlapping energy fields. We cannot separate ourselves from all that is living because *we are part of that life*, one and the same. Just so, the mind and the soul are connected. Whether we wish to or not, we cannot separate them.

When physicists conduct an experiment, they take into account what is called the *observer effect,* or the effect of the observer on the observed. The very act of observing alters what is being observed, which affects the outcome of an experiment. Similarly, in a therapeutic situation, the therapist is never truly objective. Rather, she is living part of the therapeutic moment, affecting it both verbally and nonverbally. Our bodies, minds and souls all arrive at the therapist's office, where they encounter those same aspects of the therapist. Everyone who is in the room, is in the room. There is no escaping that fact. Each person needs to be present and accounted for so each can encounter the other fully. Treating one or two aspects, but handling the third as if it does not exist, is not healthy or natural. Separating the mind from the soul and asking the two to operate independently of one another is a recipe for unhappiness, for feeling lost to other parts of ourselves, strangers in our own psyches.

> *We can perhaps summon up the courage for the possibility of a "psychology with the psyche"—that is, of a field of study based on the assumption of our autonomous psyche.*
>
> Carl Jung

> *As is the human body, so is the cosmic body. As is the human mind, so is the cosmic mind. As is the microcosm, so is the macrocosm. As is the atom, so is the universe.*
>
> The Upanishads

❦

Care of the soul is not a solving of the puzzle of life; quite the opposite, it is an appreciation of the paradoxical mysteries that blend light and darkness into the grandeur of what human life and culture can be....
Let us imagine care of the soul, then, as an appreciation of poetics in everyday life. What we want to do here is to re-imagine those things we already understand.

Thomas Moore

SOUL AWARENESS

and if i ever touched a life, i hope that life knows, that i know, that touching was is and always will be the only true revolution.

nikki giovanni

Soul is part and particle of all that exists. It is one and the same with the origin of all life. To be in touch with soul is to be connected with the source of life and consciousness.

Generally we go through life feeling either like a somebody or a nobody. Most often we interpret a person's somebody-ness through material eyes. If people possess those objects and qualities that we value as a society, we consider them somebodies. But if you ask the somebodies of this world how they feel deep in their hearts, they might admit that being somebody in the eyes of the world does not necessarily keep them from feeling like nobody within themselves. The feeling of being somebody, of being connected to something greater than the self, cannot come only from an object or an outside identity. It comes from within, from a connection with soul and life. Each of us needs to feel that we belong, that we are a part of and connected to something larger than ourselves.

> *I am certain that after the dust of centuries has passed over the cities, we, too, will be remembered not for victories or defeats in battle or in politics, but for our contribution to the human spirit.*
>
> John F. Kennedy

This is what soul awareness gives us, that sense of being connected to life in a fundamental way. It allows us to feel joy and celebrate the simple gift of life, the act of living. When we are not alone, the vicissitudes of life do not seem greater than the sense of beauty and aliveness that we gain from feeling connected to the soul.

Soul awareness is the simplest and most effective way to change society. Endlessly we struggle to get it right, to change the world so that finally we will be free of our fear of being nobody. But society will always be subject to the shifting social and political elements. What is right on one day, will be wrong the next. When we identify with the shifting sands of time and hang our sense of well-being on them, our sense of well-being shifts along with each changing circumstance. The only true liberation from the gnawing sense of things never being right is to move into an awareness of soul, a reverence for all living things, an awe of the process and the beauty of living.

Each of us has a right to feel valuable. Each of us has a right to claim the life of the soul and to make it personal. When this happens, nothing is ever the same again. If there has been a true transformation, a genuine awareness of soul integrated into us, then life will be changed both fundamentally and in a thousand ordinary ways.

This shift in perception will do more to alter society, more to alter the world than any other single act, because when we feel good about ourselves, we value others and our world. Hatred arises when we feel negative about ourselves. When it is too painful to hate ourselves in isolation, we turn the hatred outward onto everything and anything. When an inner transformation takes place and we come to see ourselves and our lives as valuable, then that is the feeling that gets turned outward toward the world. When love is turned out toward the world, society changes.

The awareness of soul is available and possible to accomplish at all time. To live alienated from this awareness is to be cast out from the Garden of Eden. But to be in the living presence of the soul is truly to return home.

❧

If you choose, you can experience yourself in a state of unity with everything you contact. In ordinary waking consciousness, you touch your finger to a rose and feel it as solid, but in truth one bundle of energy and information—your finger—is contacting another bundle of energy and information—the rose. Your finger and the thing it touches are both just minute outcroppings of the infinite field we call the universe.

Deepak Chopra, M.D.

BONDING WITH THE SOUL

What's in the Way

Reflection: First allow yourself to contemplate what a higher power might mean for you. Visualize and describe that energy using any image that feels right for you. Observe what thoughts, blocks or preconceptions arise that inhibit your ability to make a trusting and open connection with this higher aspect of self or soul. Answer the following questions in your mind or in your journal:

- Which of these blocks or inhibitions seem unnecessary or even ridiculous to you?
- Which can you release right now?
- Which feels too big to release and move out of your way?

Journal: In your journal or imagination talk directly to the block that feels too big to release and tell it why you feel you cannot move it out of your way. Say everything you want to say directly to any of the blocks. Tell them how they feel to you. Describe them in as much detail as necessary. For example, "You are my doubt. You are large, heavy and you make me feel like a fool for believing in anything I can't see."

When you have said everything you need to say, say goodbye to the blocks and release them.

Now, what would you like to say to a higher power, or to your soul nature? Write or imagine whatever feels appropriate.

BONDING WITH THE SOUL

THE WORD SOUL

Reflection: Relax, get comfortable. Answer these questions in your mind or journal:

- When I hear the word soul, I think of _____.
- When I try to imagine a person with soul, I see _____.
- The aspect of soul that makes me uncomfortable is _____.
- Soul and my day-to-day life seem _____.
- If I let soul work in my life, it might make me _____.
- My religious experience was _____.
- What my religion made me feel about soul was _____.
- A soulful moment is _____.
- I sense soul in my life when _____.
- To deepen my relationship with soul, I need more _____.
- An activity that connects me with soul is _____.

Journal: Choose a few of the questions that speak the loudest to you and answer them more fully.

3
Family

THE SOUL AND THE HOME

I laugh when I hear the fish in the water is thirsty. You don't grasp the fact that what is most alive of all is inside your own house, and so you walk from one holy city to the next with a confused look! Kabir will tell you the truth: go wherever you like, to Calcutta or Tibet; if you can't find where your soul is hidden, for you the world will never be real!

Robert Bly

A good home creates a container in which the ordinary soul can be held and nurtured. A loving, stable home provides a warm context in which the soul can safely arise into the experience of day-to-day living, a place to enjoy the company of other souls. A true home is a center that we can move away from and return to, a safe harbor in which we can drop anchor and allow ourselves to enjoy the waters that surround us. We can take risks in the world outside, knowing that we have a home to drift back to.

Home is also where we engage with those who are closest to us—our parents, grandparents, spouses, children, partners, friends. At its best, home is a "safe house" where we can love, fight, make up, mess up, clean up, just plain live in the certainty that we will not be forever banned for our transgressions.

Unfortunately, sometimes we think of home as a place to keep our possessions rather than a place of commingling spirits. There is a great difference between how it feels to walk into a house that feels like a home, and to walk into a house that feels like a furniture showroom. For all too many people, home means cold rather than warmth, being kept at arm's length rather than being embraced.

A home is a place that can nurture soul growth, a place where we are not afraid to be. We all need a home and a sense of connectedness with those around us. We all need to feel that there is a well to go to for water, a spring from which we can drink when thirsty, a container in which we can experience soul.

It is my feeling that development is biologically programmed, and tied to this is the parent-child bonding and learning process. I believe that from early childhood through adolescence, children are most open to parental teaching. Our children are most receptive to the vital information we need to share with them in these years before the process of separation. Young children are deeply open to their parents, in fact they idealize them. What is taught in these years has immense staying power. What we as parents give them during this time is a gift for life. It is difficult to redo or make up for what does not happen in the parent-child relationship during the child's youth; and happily it is equally difficult to undo the love, care and attention given by a parent from birth through adolescence. It is the truest gift of the soul.

🌿

There is nothing like staying at home for real comfort.

Jane Austen

FROM MOTHER TO SELF

The mother's lap is the child's first classroom.

Hindu proverb

From the moment of conception a child grows, not only within the body of her mother, but within her total inner world. From birth to nine months, the child does not really distinguish a difference between self and mother; mother and child are a world containing one.

Along with this sense of oneness, a child can feel that her life is at risk when separated from her mother, because the separation feels like division from the self. By nine months, however, a child begins to recognize that her spirit is contained in a body detached from Mother's. She can look at herself and look back at Mother and realize in amazement that the two are not one and the same.

This sense of oneness in the earliest stage of life is natural and crucial for a child's healthy development. To be fully identified with her mother allows a child to be bonded not only to Mother, but with her own soul as it expresses itself through her body. This is nature's way of allowing the spirit to become flesh. Mother, rather than being an end point in this process, is a passage through which her soul passes on its road to individuation. Slowly, in small increments, the child learns to self-define, learns that she is a separate being complete unto herself, with her own inner will and volition, mind and heart.

Because a child at first experiences herself as the same as her mother, there are times of confusion. This is most evident in the adolescent who constantly sends out signals to Mother to keep away. During this period, Mother's response is crucial to how her child transfers her mother's self and incorporates it into her own self, into her own center.

One of the effects of feeling at one with her child is that Mother, too, experiences an almost divine sense of belonging to something larger than herself. She experiences herself entwined in the child's self. When her child separates, there can also be considerable identity confusion on Mother's part. She may feel, "Who am I if I am not my child's mother?"

The mother who lacks a strong sense of self may resent her child's wish to have her own life and may punish her in a variety of small ways for attempting to be independent. Unconsciously she may deny her child the right to take her maternal love and security and incorporate it into herself to use as an inner source of love and strength on her journey. The child who incorporates a resentful mother will find that she has taken in an unloving presence. When the child goes to her internalized mother to be soothed, rather than soothing she may hear punitive and harsh messages. On the other hand, the mother who can allow her child to incorporate her loving presence within and take it with her when she moves into her life journey, gives an inner spring from which to draw waters that refresh and nurture and sustain life.

Respect the child. Be not too much his parent. Trespass not on his solitude.

Ralph Waldo Emerson

Metaphorically, the child carries in her heart a suitcase for her life journey packed by her mother. What she needs to find in this suitcase is unconditional love and positive regard. If, when she looks for inspiration and strength, she finds failure, disrespect and her mother's wish never to let go, she will find guilt and pain instead.

Successful and happy incorporation of the mother, from the self of the mother to the self of the child, or working through the pain of a less than successful incorporation is one of the most important steps on the path toward soul realization. Freely given maternal love and positive regard, with no strings attached, are the deepest richness we can have. As a society we have grossly undervalued a profoundly important role, that of mother, and we have undermined woman's ability to feel good about the role, making her feel that being a mother is not enough. It is not the role that needs to be changed, but the esteem in which we hold it. A good mother is the treasure of a lifetime.

❦

*If you bungle raising your children,
nothing else much matters in life.*

Jacqueline Kennedy Onassis

FROM FATHER TO SELF

If there is anything we wish to change in the child, we should first examine it and see whether it is not something that could better be changed in ourselves.

Carl Jung

I have a place that I go in my mind: I sit on the balcony of my childhood home with my father, where I first understood consciously what love felt like. I arose each day, and always he was there. He introduced the dawn to me; he was morning itself. He lifted me onto the counter and talked to me as I watched him squeeze fresh orange juice. I felt that his hands were magical, that love was made to live in them. Then he made cafe au lait in a glass, and we sat together on the balcony to usher in morning. He always brought a special spoon to give me sips of coffee, blowing on it carefully to make sure it wasn't too hot.

I felt adored by my father. He took me on excursions, little walks down the block, shopping at the fish market, where we bought something special and brought it home to cook. We went hunting for dandelion greens. And all the while he visited with me, explained the world to me and told me stories about himself when he was young. He seemed always interested in what was on my mind, and he taught me to come forward with my innermost thoughts. If he saw sadness on my face, he asked me what was wrong. He made me feel valuable.

He worried about me when I was upset and he celebrated with me when I was happy. He taught me what love felt like. It was with this inner knowledge that I chose a life partner. When I experienced this feeling again, I knew deep within me that this was the man I wanted to spend my life with. We are taught love in this way and we teach love in this way. When we have learned love, we know what love is when we experience it again. The parent teaches not by what he says but by who he is. Modeling is the most profound level of learning passed on from parent to child. A father who loves himself, his wife and his children will teach a son to do the same without ever saying a word on the subject. A father who loves his daughter will teach her that she deserves the love and respect of a good man.

The internalized father, like the internalized mother, is carried within the child into adulthood. It is important to understand the position of the father within the family because that is how the father may be positioned within the self. For instance, a father who was distant and emotionally removed may be internalized in that way by the child, so she will have within her an emotionally distant and removed paternal aspect or voice. When, as an the adult, she turns inward for fatherly counsel, strength and support, she will find instead what she got. She will feel again as she felt then.

Spending a lifetime working to gain the blessing or approval of the internalized father is not an unusual pattern. A withheld paternal blessing can make people overachieve or cause them to give up feeling that they will ever do enough or be enough to deserve to succeed and be happy. The blessing of the father, freely and lovingly given, helps to create an inner fortitude and strength, courage to take one's place in the world.

❦

When one has not had a good father, one must create one.

Friedrich Nietzsche

INTERGENERATIONAL LIVING

*Emancipation from the bondage of the soil
is no freedom for the tree.*

Rabindranath Tagore

Today most of us live in peer ghettos—families with children in one neighborhood, young singles in another, elders in their own closed community. We have neatly prevented ourselves from getting the cross-fertilization provided by the interaction of two or three generations, which helps us feel stable and grounded. When elders are not present, the next two generations do not get the nurturing and guidance they need. When wisdom and tools for living do not get passed from one generation to the next, the wisdom and tools disappear.

Intergenerational living follows nature's life-course pattern, allowing each generation to get what it needs to feel whole and happy. The oldest generation is able to pass down what they have learned, mentoring those behind them, as well as having in a sense a living life review surrounding them.

According to psychologist Erik Erikson, reviewing one's life is a part of the developmental task of our final years. Older people who understand how to be elders, who are able to pass on encouragement and strength rather than despair and judgment, are gifts to society. Elders who have worked through their own failures and inadequacies and come to terms with their lives are able to mentor without controlling, give advice without criticism, and help people who are younger to get in touch with their own strength, their own soul.

My grandmother is still living, and one of my favorite moments in life is when I walk up to her back door, ring the bell and stand waiting for her to open the door and greet me. I hear a loud squeak as the door opens and the familiar touch and smell of Grammie's house surrounds me. She will make a cup of coffee for me and, if I like, half a piece of toast, and we will sit and talk. If it is near a mealtime, we will eat together and go over the latest news.

I am one of the lucky ones. This experience has been available to me all my life. I have had the profound good fortune of having a grandmother who understands how to play her role and the deep importance of her role. Through everything that has happened in my life, I have always been able to count on my grandmother. She is always happy to see me, has time to listen to what is on my mind and makes me feel like somebody, like I have a place held safe for me in this world. She, in turn, is not afraid to need us and does not pretend to be an island unto herself, independent of the need for love and support. When we get together and I tell her how good it is to be with her, she says the same thing: "Its good for me, it's good for all of us, we all need this."

When I had my first child, there was no one I would rather spend time with than Grammie. I liked carrying my daughter around with me and being with her all the time. I raised my children when women were supposedly being liberated from household life, but liberation for me meant the freedom to be with them. It was my grandmother who constantly said, "Sweetheart, you're doing it the right way. We did it the wrong way; you're doing a beautiful job." She would take delight with me in my little ones, enjoying their behavior, recognizing their strengths, not avoiding their weaknesses and helping me learn how to mother them. She taught me that parenting is too important and overwhelming a task for one generation, that parents need help, they need parenting themselves. They need other loving people to care about their children, not just physically but spiritually and emotionally, to love their children as they do, to take joy in their upward movement and feel sorrow when trouble comes.

She also gave me the great gift of continuity by telling me countless stories of her life with her husband of 50 years. She taught me that life was hard but beautiful, that family was complicated but necessary and worthwhile, and that though marriage was full of ups and downs, it was a great source of love and security and personal growth. I have never seen anyone laugh as long and as hard as my grandmother; her best laughs are at herself. She models the meaning of being human and alive, being present and a carrier of history, being a walking amplification of soul.

Generations are connected to one another seamlessly, each leading naturally into the next. The old receive the vitality of youth, the youth the stability of the old, and the middle the nurturing to meet the demands of day-to-day living. All are nurtured, all receive what they need. The tools we need to live our lives grow stronger as they are passed through the generations, from hand to hand to hand.

❧

To be happy in this world, especially when youth is past, it is necessary to feel oneself not merely an isolated individual whose day will soon be over, but part of the stream of life flowing on from the first germ to the remote and unknown future.

Bertrand Russell

ACCOUNTABILITY

It is a common experience in the world for people to get along and function well in their network relationships in the world and poorly in their families. They are unhooked, less invested, more objective and expect less from their network of friends and workers. If people would examine how well they function in some areas of their life and make the equivalent translation to their close family relationships, they would improve their function in the family one hundred percent. Expectations may get the job done but the emotional climate is stifling. Decades from now we will all be dead. What will it matter if the beds were made or unmade. . . . What will matter and influence people long after we are gone is the emotional legacy that we leave to our children and through them to their children. This will have influence when we are all forgotten. It is these unworkable levels of expectation, largely transmitted through the generations, that turn people off.

Thomas Fogarty, M.D.

One of the potential pitfalls of the therapeutic process is to get stuck in blaming our family of origin for all our problems. Much of who we are is profoundly shaped by the family in which we were raised, but that is not the entire story. When we seek all of the explanations for who we are in our parental influences and use our discovery as excuses for giving up on love, we disempower our souls. The purpose of going back into our family of origin, which is a vital and necessary part of the therapeutic process, is to reclaim the parts of ourselves that we left behind and bring them into the present. As this is being accomplished, we continue simultaneously to move on in our own lives.

To free ourselves from self-hatred and loathing, we need to understand where accountability lies. For example, a child who is brought up in an alcoholic or abusive home will tend to blame her-

Accusing the times is but excusing ourselves.

English proverb

self for what went wrong in her family. Because, as children, we feel responsible and do not have the power to differentiate ourselves from our parents and siblings, we tend to internalize the pain and dysfunction in our homes as our fault. We live with the illusion that if we could change, if we could become better children, our parents would like us better and the anger and sadness around us would disappear. We become self-hating and self-blaming.

Making parents and other family members accountable for our behavior helps our recovery by externalizing the blame so we can stop beating up on ourselves. At some point in the therapeutic process, the anger and hatred that has been irrationally directed inward will also be irrationally directed outward, toward those who perpetrated the abuse. This is a natural part of the healing process, but it is not the entire healing process. *We are more than our parents. We are more than our families.* Our parents and families are vehicles through which we learn to see ourselves. Eventually we will have to take responsibility for who we are and where we are in our lives.

According to Mahatma Gandhi, our most significant battles are fought in the privacy of our own hearts, in our true encounter with ourselves. This is not far from the psychoanalytic concept of gaining a sense of mastery over a trauma: fighting the battle on the inside so that we do not continually recreate the problem in our lives. In each case we are working toward some sense of reempowerment and meaning, even if that deeper understanding leads us only to our own essential sense of powerlessness over circumstance. When we arrive at a sense of powerlessness through wisdom rather than defeat, we can come to terms with what we can control and what we must let go of. We recognize our own need to accept what *is*, rather than what we wish could be. We are no longer trapped on the ever-spinning wheel of action and reaction, blaming others for problems that no one has caused. Only when we stop holding others accountable for all of our troubles can we truly be free.

※

In short, the soul-journey resembles very much the sort of adventure one encounters in folklore and myth. According to archaic view, all men apparently have the chance to become a sort of Odysseus, whether they like it or not.

Paul Zweig

BONDING WITH THE SOUL

PHOTOGRAPHS

Reflection: Slowly walk around some photographs you have framed or that are hanging on a wall, or page slowly through photos tucked into albums. Let yourself be drawn to an image of yourself from any time of your life that speaks to you. When you have selected a special photograph, hold it in your hands and look at it carefully. How do you sense that you felt in this picture? What do you feel you would like to be saying? What do you feel you would like to do?

Journal: First, reverse roles with yourself in the photograph and write a journal entry as the person in the picture, saying everything you feel you would have liked to say then but were not able to. Write in the first person, referring to yourself with a name or nickname you used then, i.e., "My name is Bobbie. I am eight and I have long brown hair. I am sitting here, etc." When you have finished, reverse roles back to yourself today and write a message or share some wisdom with the you that is in the photograph. What would you like to tell yourself then from your present-day self that you had no way of knowing when you were younger? What do you wish you knew then that you know now? Why do you think this photograph is of particular meaning to you?

BONDING WITH THE SOUL

FAMILY MYTHOLOGY

Reflection: We can spend a lifetime attempting to live up to myths. Remember, myths aren't falsehoods, but our family's attempt to explain itself to itself or to the world. For example, a family myth might be the belief that a close family is a family where there is no conflict or fighting. Another myth might be that if a couple is close, they like to do all the same things together, and so on. Let's explore what we might have accepted as true—whether it was or not—and how we are living it out today. In your mind, or in your journal, fill in the missing word at the end of these sentences.

- If my family had a motto, it would be _____.
- During quiet moments we felt _____.
- My family gave high praise to _____.
- The three strongest values held by my family were _____,
_____, _____.
- Generally speaking, we functioned _____.

Journal: Write a response to this in your journal. Where would your family's beliefs about itself play out in reality and what were the beliefs that had no foundation in reality? Are there any beliefs that you can identify now as myths—not borne out in reality—that you are still trying to live by today? What beliefs feel real and comfortable in your life today? What beliefs feel false and exist only as a myth?

4
Relationships

THE CRUCIBLE OF RELATIONSHIP

Every moment of our life is relationship.
There is nothing except relationship.

Charlotte Joko Beck, *Everyday Zen*

Few situations in life are as conducive to soul-making as that of a deep, committed relationship. Generally, we choose as intimate partners people with whom we can continue our life process of finishing our unfinished selves. If our personal issues are unconscious, our choice of a partner will be ruled by these pressing unconscious needs and drives.

Unfortunately, we are rarely aware of this aspect of relationship. When we reach a place in ourselves that is too painful to look at, we see our relationship as the cause of our pain rather than own our personal issues. When the pain becomes too great, we may decide that leaving the relationship through an affair, a preoccupation with work or children, or even a divorce is a good way to solve our pain.

Sometimes leaving a relationship truly is the only solution, but there are countless other times when leaving the relationship means leaving our own deep personal issues untouched and unresolved. Intimacy and commitment act as triggers to bring up all of our fears of vulnerability, dependency, exposure and abandonment. Moving through these fears, experiencing them for what they are and integrating them into our total being, allows us to center ourselves within our own soul natures. Painful as they are to face, our unresolved issues help us move down the path toward soul experience.

In a society that has added two or three decades to the lifespan, the vow "till death do us part" has changed in meaning and length. Today, if we are choosing a life partner, we are choosing someone with whom we will raise children and grandchildren, then possibly go on to spend another two or three decades of life. Because the needs and demands on the couple will change radically from one period of life to another relationships must be extremely flexible. All relationships are hard work. A deep, committed relationship will call on us to do more soul searching than probably any single area of our lives. This is precisely why it is so useful in the development of the soul nature and the removing of obstacles that are in the way of soul nature: because it reaches into our unconscious in a way that few experiences of life do, demanding all of us. And when we feel we are tired and cannot go on any longer, it asks for more.

In our society we have come to see relationships as something from which we should expect a great deal, and when we don't get what we want, we may feel we have compromised ourselves, that we are "settling for less," being weak or lacking in self-respect. But if this is our attitude, we are missing an important function of relationship. *The continuity and history of a long-term relationship is the crucible in which we can melt down the lead we carry in our psyches and transform it into the gold of the soul.* The relationship that triggers unfinished issues gives us the opportunity to resolve them and move on. Living with another person day in and day out gives us the opportunity to learn the value of give and take. Perhaps most important, we may learn the lesson of compassion: that treating the other well is treating ourselves well, and treating ourselves well is treating the other well.

❧

Only in relationships can you know yourself, not in abstraction and certainly not in isolation. The movement of behavior is the sure guide to yourself, it's the mirror of your consciousness; this mirror will reveal its content, the images, the attachments, the fears, the loneliness, the joy and sorrow. Poverty lies in running away from this, either in its sublimations or its identities.

J. Krishnamurti

READER/CUSTOMER CARE SURVEY

If you are enjoying this book, please help us serve you better and meet your changing needs by taking a few minutes to complete this survey. Please fold it & drop it in the mail.
As a thank you, we will send you a gift.

Name: _____

Address: _____

_____

Tel. # _____

Gender: ____ Female ____ Male

Age: ____ 18-25   ____ 46-55
____ 26-35   ____ 56-65
____ 36-45   ____ 65+

Marital Status: ____ Married ____ Single
____ Divorced ____ Partner

Is this book: ____ Purchase for self?
____ Purchase for others?
____ Received as gift?

How did you find out about this book?

____ Catalog
____ Store Display
Newspaper
____ Best Seller List
____ Article/Book Review
____ Advertisement
Magazine
____ Feature Article
____ Book Review
____ Advertisement
____ Word of Mouth
____ T.V./Talk Show (Specify) _____
____ Radio/Talk Show (Specify) _____
____ Professional Referral _____
____ Other (Specify) _____

What subject areas do you enjoy reading most? (Rank in order of enjoyment)

____ Women's Issues   ____ New Age
____ Business Self Help   ____ Aging
____ Relationships   ____ Altern. Healing
____ Inspiration   ____ Parenting
____ Soul/Spirituality   ____ Diet/Nutrition
____ Recovery   ____ Exercise/Health
____ Other (Specify) _____

What do you look for when choosing a personal growth book? (Rank in order of importance)

____ Subject   ____ Author
____ Title   ____ Price
____ Cover Design ____ In Store Location
____ Other (Specify) _____

When do you buy books? (Rank in order of importance)

____ Xmas   ____ Father's Day
____ Valentines Day ____ Summer Reading
____ Birthday   ____ Thanksgiving
____ Mother's Day
____ Other (Specify) _____

Where do you buy your books? (Rank in order of frequency of purchases)

____ Bookstore   ____ Book Club
____ Price Club   ____ Mail Order
____ Department Store ____ T.V. Shopping
____ Supermarket   ____ Airport
____ Health Food Store ____ Drug Store
____ Gift Store   ____ Other (Specify)

Additional comments you would like to make to help us serve you better.

_____

_____

_____

3391/250

Thank You ii

NO POSTAGE
NECESSARY
IF MAILED
IN THE
UNITED STATES

BUSINESS REPLY MAIL

FIRST CLASS MAIL PERMIT NO 45 DEERFIELD BEACH, FL

POSTAGE WILL BE PAID BY ADDRESSEE

HEALTH COMMUNICATIONS
3201 SW 15TH STREET
DEERFIELD BEACH, FL 33442-9875

THE GOOD ENOUGH RELATIONSHIP

Seldom, or perhaps never, does a marriage develop into an individual relationship smoothly and without crises, there is no coming to consciousness without pain.

Carl Jung

When we can bring our full being to a relationship without feeling that we have to hide a part of ourselves, we have a real chance to use relationship as a pathway to soul. Sometimes, however, we ask more of relationship than it can give and thus doom ourselves to disappointment. Just as D.W. Winnicott speaks of the "good enough" parent, I would like to propose that there is such a thing as a "good enough" relationship. A relationship cannot be all things. If it successfully enough provides what we need to go on in our life process of personal development—feeling loved and a sense of basic security—it is *good enough*.

Life is long, if we are lucky, and any long-term relationship will have its ups and downs. If we are perfectionistic and see every down as a complete failure of the relationship, we will not have the perspective necessary to stay with the relationship and work through that period into another, more satisfying one. If we see all life problems as relationship problems, we will see the solution to life problems as leaving one relationship and find-

What a miserable thing life is; you're living in clover only the clover isn't good enough.

Bertholt Brecht

ing another. When we do this, we don't necessarily simplify our lives; often, we make them more complicated. Before we give up, it may make more sense to see if the problem can be resolved within the self and within the relationship.

We enter relationships with many myths: We will not feel lonely when we have a relationship; we will always have someone to count on; we will feel fulfilled inside all the time when we have a relationship; a good relationship does not have problems. These seductive myths can send us into despair whenever we encounter the difficulties, strains and pains that are so natural in a partnership. They can also make us demand things from a relationship that are unrealistic, or even make us abandon a relationship before it has a chance to grow into all that it can be. No one person can be all things to another person. We have enough work to do sorting out ourselves. When we allow ourselves to be with the flow we are able to stay with the relationship. If something is wrong, we will sense it and go about correcting it and if not, we will leave it alone.

Relationships are not static. When we make them conform to a perception rather than just be, in a sense we leave the relationship and enter an image. Then we feel empty and set about looking for the relationship in all the wrong places. It didn't go anywhere, we did. Good, bad or indifferent, the relationship is only what is happening in the moment. When we divide ourselves from the moment, we divide ourselves from the soul of the relationship. When we can learn what a relationship can give us, and what is unfair or inappropriate to expect of one another, we are free to go about our personal development with the loving support of partners. Then, rather than making them antagonists in our lives, we allow them to become lifelong friends. And this is good enough.

ᘞ

It is better to get rid of the problem and keep the person than to get rid of the person and keep the problem.

Harville Hendrix

LOVE/HATE

There is no fruit that is not bitter before it is ripe.

Publilius Syrus

The summer my daughter was eight we took a family trip. One day we were gathered on the shore of a large lake, taking turns water skiing. When I was skiing away and out of vision, my daughter, an adorable innocent little girl with sweet pigtails, turned to my husband and said, "I wish Mommy would fall down and the sharks would come and eat her and I would see the bone." Then she continued to watch me, smiling, playing in the sand and saying, "Look at Mommy." My husband, who was holding her hand at the time, was rather taken aback. He turned to her and said something like, "That might hurt Mommy." My daughter seemed relatively unaffected by this thought and continued playing.

There are a couple of forces at work here—at least. One is the natural expression of hate toward the person you love and depend upon the most. The other is the child's wish to get rid of the same sex parent so that she will have the opposite sex parent to herself. Both of these are natural feelings on the part of the child. Accepting them helps the child to be less fearful of her own feelings. Then she can move beyond them and become free of their unconscious grip, so that they do not contaminate relationships later in life.

All children harbor destructive wishes towards their parents. Both love and hate are a part of the child's feeling world. When she can discover that she does not have the power to destroy her parents' love or presence in her life, even though at times she may wish to, she can integrate both of these feelings within herself as being a natural part of any deep intimate relationship. When she cannot, when she is forced by circumstance to relegate negative feelings to her unconscious, those feelings may find expression in passive-aggressive or otherwise destructive ways. They may even be turned against the self, where they will confuse the child and make her guilty over what she carries in the silence of her mind. She will be forced to split off from a part of herself.

Unintegrated feelings from childhood carry over into intimate relationships throughout life. We all know people who can acknowledge only one aspect of self, who are unable to see, for example, negative qualities in a spouse because those qualities seem too threatening. Their unconscious fear that if they allow themselves to see the negative qualities and feel the feelings, they will destroy the relationship, keeps them in denial. The problem may be that they were never really allowed to see these aspects of their own parents, to learn in childhood that these feelings were natural. Eventually, for any deep intimate relationship to survive, it will need to accommodate the good and the bad, the liked with the disliked. This is how deep relationships can remain alive and people can continue to grow within them. Otherwise the relationship tends to become role-typed and stratified. People who are happy together have generally learned to accommodate the whole of the person to whom they are related, which allows the soul of the relationship to flow more freely.

Love does not cause suffering;
what causes it is the sense of ownership,
which is love's opposite.

Antoine de Saint-Exupéry

THE INTERRELATIONSHIP OF ALL THINGS

We had the idea that the human was somehow separate from the universe and the scientist would view his or her work as observing the universe from afar. . . . Now we can't hold that dualism any more. . . . From the very beginning, in a sense, the universe was poised to bring forth life, so our existence here can't be seen as something that's alien. And, furthermore, our own deep experiences, the realm of the psyche, the soul, the feelings of the human, this too is as much a part of the universe as the stars are of the gravitational interaction. It is a primary illustration of the underlying order of the universe.

Brian Swimm

We may think we know what a relationship is, but the new world view of quantum mechanics, which sees all matter and energy as interrelated, asks us to look again. Freud's period in history was influenced by a Newtonian world view that saw people as separate objects relating to other separate objects. In the traditional therapeutic situation, then, one person is seen as being more objective than the other, or as somehow able to separate from the reality of the situation and observe as if from afar. But quantum mechanics tells us that separation in this sense is not possible. Inevitably, we influence whatever situation we are in, and it in turn influences us. We are all a part of the same alive environment, constantly interacting and overlapping in all conscious and unconscious elements of the atmosphere. Dianne Zohar makes this clear: "If you apply the wave particle metaphor to human relationship and think that we are both particle, individuals in our own space and time and

> *The influence of the senses has in most men overpowered the minds to that degree that the walls of time and space have come to look real and insurmountable; and to speak with levity of these limits is, in this world, the sign of insanity. Yet time and space are but inverse measures of the force of the soul.*
>
> Ralph Waldo Emerson

waves, things that can overlap and combine with others, then you have a basis for seeing how we could get *into* relationships with other people."

Relationship in this sense shares the same life and soul as the people who are in the relationship. There is me, there is you and then there is the acknowledgment of the me-you space. Relationship has a life of its own in the overlap of energy. Seen this way, a block in the relationship is never one-sided. It will be experienced by both people. This does not mean that we lose the self in relationship. If we have a secure self, that is, if we know our own self, we can blend it with the other's secure self to create a third entity and still tell one from the other. Paradoxically perhaps, one of the ways to find ourselves in relationship lies in our ability to temporarily lose the self without disintegrating.

In India there is a beautiful greeting. People put their palms together over their heart, bow their heads slightly and say, "Namaste," which means, "I pray to the divinity within you." This greeting acknowledges that each one of us is connected through the same force or energy; that at the truest, deepest level, we are one.

Learn to see God in all persons, of whatever race or creed. You will know what divine love is when you begin to feel your oneness with every human being, not before. In mutual service we forget the little self and glimpse the one measureless self, the spirit that unifies all men.

Parmahansa Yogananda

BONDING WITH THE SOUL

INTIMATE RELATIONSHIPS

Reflection: Relax, get comfortable, and allow a problem or concern that occurs repeatedly in an intimate relationship to come to mind. Let the situation unfold in your mind's eye and let yourself feel whatever feelings come with it. Then in your mind or your journal, answer these questions:

- ❦ What words describe or capture how you feel at these times?
- ❦ Can you recall feeling like that before, and with whom?
- ❦ If you could say something now that you couldn't say before to that person, what would it be?
- ❦ Returning now to the present, do you see any correlation between your current situation and the past?
- ❦ What is it?
- ❦ How might the previous situation be affecting your current one?

Journal: In your journal, divide a page into three columns. At the top of the first column, write "Present"; the middle column, "Feelings"; the third column, "Past." In the first column describe briefly as many situations as you choose that occur regularly in your intimate relationships that you find problematic. In the second column, corresponding to each situation, write words that describe how you feel when that situation occurs. In the third column, write situations from your past intimate or family relationships in which you felt those same feelings. Then look at your columns. Are there meaningful connections between what happened in the past and how the past might be influencing how you experience the present?

BONDING WITH THE SOUL

UNFINISHED BUSINESS

Reflection: Be seated, close your eyes, quiet your mind and allow to come into your mind a person with whom you have unfinished business. It might be an intimate relationship that has never come to a comfortable closure, or a relationship that still lives inside of you in an unfinished state. When that person is in your mind, allow yourself to feel the suspended emotions that you carry within you.

Journal: When that person with whom you feel you have unfinished business is clearly in your mind and the feelings related to the relationship are clear, write a letter to him or her. Express every feeling and thought you want this person to hear. Put on paper all the thoughts and feelings, positive and negative, you didn't or couldn't communicate clearly in the past. Sign the letter. Read it, then fold it and put it away because it's for your use only, or possibly share it with a trusted person.

5
Forgiveness and Letting Go

FORGIVENESS AND LETTING GO

If your brother sins, call him to task, and if he repents, forgive him.

Luke 17:3

Rather than an act of will, forgiveness and letting go is a process. It takes time, it requires patience and comes, not necessarily when we wish it, but when we are ready. We can't really forgive another until first we have forgiven ourselves. Though it may look as if forgiveness has been arrived at spontaneously, upon closer reflection we see we have passed through specific stages in order to prepare for the final outcome of forgiveness. To be self-mindful long enough to process our barriers is the deepest challenge of forgiveness. Outlined here is the course that these stages can follow. Though the order may vary, as can the length of time spent in any one stage, we will more or less need to move through the full process on our path toward forgiving and letting go. These stages are like layers of an onion in that they are interdependent and interactive. They can be cycled through for each emotional block or issue being processed.

Stage One: Making the unconscious conscious/Anger and hurt
- work through denial, shame and guilt
- feel the full impact of the circumstance or relationship on one's life
- move from blaming self to feeling anger toward the other, from victimization to empowerment
- feel hurt and anger at a conscious level rather than act it out in destructive ways

Stage Two: Despair and mourning/Separating the past from the present

- mourn the loss, process feeling the futility, loss and waste of what could have been, move from acting out the pain to feeling it
- become aware that "it wasn't me after all," "it wasn't my fault."
- become aware of how yesterday's pain is contaminating life today, live more fully in the present
- move from connection, through enmeshment, to genuine mutual connection

Stage Three: Acceptance/Letting go
- come to terms with loss/"life isn't fair"
- begin to accept and forgive the self, let go of self-hatred and self-blame
- let go of the need to re-enact the trauma
- allow life to feel good, take a leap of faith

Stage Four: Compassion/Forgiveness
- psychologically reverse roles with the other person and see the situation through his or her eyes
- the dawning of the ability to find meaning in what happened
- learn lessons about life, learn to live with feeling good

STAGE ONE

Making the Unconscious Conscious/Anger and Hurt

What a wee little part of a person's life are his acts and his words! His real life is led in his head, and is known to none but himself.

Mark Twain

None of us wants to think that those we depend on for love and companionship would hurt us, or that we would or have hurt someone else. Letting go of denial means that we have to live with the

The shell must break before the bird can fly.

Alfred, Lord Tennyson

whole truth, to sit with it (spend time with it), to feel it, to risk the pain and disillusionment of *knowing*. Allowing ourselves to feel the full impact of how a person or circumstance has influenced our lives in painful ways is an initial step in eventually heal-

The Child is father of the Man.

William Wordsworth

ing from it. In a sense, this is a stage of diagnosis: allowing ourselves to see the wound so we can understand what we are working with. It is for this reason that this stage is so painful. In fact, many people have trouble making it through this initial stage of forgiveness. Letting go of denial, then, is seeing and feeling the wound.

Another block in this stage is guilt. Often we carry an irrational sense of guilt when something has gone wrong in our lives. We feel

Great is truth and strongest of all.

Apocrypha

we are somehow to blame. If we had been different, we could have prevented this pain. We must have done something

God offers to every mind its choice between truth and repose.

Ralph Waldo Emerson

wrong. Beneath these feelings can lie an even deeper feeling of shame. Not only did we *do* something wrong, but we *are* something wrong. "Something must be wrong with me as a person, or none of this would have happened. Trouble chose me for a reason."

Healing requires feeling this guilt and shame. Experiencing shame is very difficult. It takes courage, humility and self-awareness to sit with shame without either denying it or in some way running from the feeling. If we can hold ourselves in a compassionate light and actually tolerate these very difficult feelings, the wheels of self-love and forgiveness can be set into motion.

A road that does not lead to other roads always has to be retraced, unless the traveler wishes to rust at the end of it.

Tehyi Hsich

Feeling the extent of our anger and hurt is a necessary step on the path to forgiveness. It is a common occurrence to turn inward on ourselves the anger that we do not feel safe expressing toward another person. Hating ourselves or carrying feelings of self-loathing isolates us, undermines our ability to make meaningful connections or to reach out toward others, and can also lead to depression. The anger may get mixed up with guilt. Feeling that "it must be my fault in some way" can make us turn anger inward as a way of punishing ourselves. If we feel responsible and at fault we may create a vicious circle—i.e., the more we feel abused, the more at fault we feel and the more we turn anger inward onto ourselves. Feelings of self-loathing make us feel bad about ourselves, which can cause depression, or we may act abusively toward others in an attempt to get rid of painful emotions. It is for this reason that we must break the cycle, feel the anger and hurt, and trace it back to its source. It is giving voice to the silent scream, freeing the self from victimhood or from constant self-blame and self-flagellation. It empowers the victim to fight back, to stop *being* the problem.

A man that studieth revenge keeps his own wounds green which otherwise would heal and do well.

Francis Bacon

No man is angry that feels not himself hurt.

Francis Bacon

Abuse or depression can be the consequence of unconscious, unfelt hurt and anger. When repressed anger and hurt are brought to consciousness and felt rather than denied, it is less likely that they will be acted out unconsciously. When we are willing to take responsibility for the hurt and anger we carry, to feel and work them through, the feelings get processed rather than acted out in destructive or abusive ways. This is how to break the cycle of abuse.

❦

I learned that our fear creates our own negativity. Negativity from other people is a thought form that can certainly come into any field, but it's not going to harm me unless I allow it to. I can send it back to the person who sent it to me.

Lynn Andrews, *The Woman of Wyrrd*

STAGE TWO

DESPAIR AND MOURNING/SEPARATING THE PAST FROM THE PRESENT

Sadness flies on the wings of the morning and out of the heart of darkness comes the light.

Jean Giradoux

Once the unhealthy dynamics of a relationship or situation have become conscious and an individual has been willing to attend truly to the pain and anger, several things happen. At the start, a process of mourning is initiated when we become conscious of all that happened and are willing to feel sad. Before this, remember, the sadness was not fully felt, but was sidetracked into compulsive or neurotic behaviors. It

A deep distress hath humanized my soul.

William Wordsworth

remained unconscious, where it fueled negative behavior patterns. At this stage we mourn what happened and what never got a chance to happen, what was and what never got to be or never will be. There is a biting pain to this stage.

When we have undergone a great deal of pain, there is a secondary gain in that the pain allows us to feel alive and gives us a sense of connectedness to a person, a family or a situation. Mourning the loss, then, is also vacating this means of feeling alive and connected *before* replacing it with a new way. It is an act of faith and part of what will begin to rebuild a new kind of trust in life. During this mourning, we can feel a bone-chilling sense of aloneness.

Melancholy and remorse form the deep leaden keel which enables us to sail into the wind of reality.

Cyril Connolly

This is an individuating, self-actualizing step. It implies that we are developing enough ego strength to live without a dysfunctional connection, and releasing that resentment that may be our strongest sense of connection to another person or situation. This step declares that internal peace and contentment are worth more than a pain-filled, resentful connection.

Though this step is liberating and empowering, it is also scary. It brings into focus an existential sense of aloneness. On the path to soul, this aloneness and emptiness needs to be felt and lived with in order to make the soul connection. We need to reach out a hand from darkness and connect with the light. Though this emptiness can be disorienting and painful, experiencing it actually is very productive.

While grief is fresh, every attempt to divert it only irritates it.

Samuel Johnson

It puts us in touch with a deeper pulse of life. It allows us to stand firmly on slippery rocks and to maintain our footing even though the waters around us shift constantly.

Another awareness that this phase brings is that "it wasn't me after all," or "it wasn't my fault." What an astonishing release that realization brings. As we said earlier, guilt and shame are part of what block forgiveness. Letting go of a sense that someone must be at fault forgives the self as well as the other, and frees the energies tied up in detective work for better, more life-engendering activities. Even insurance companies find it more cost-effective to have "no fault" insurance. The massive quantities of time, energy and resources that are required in figuring out who's to blame ultimately are too costly. There are just too many extenuating circumstances to reduce it to culpability and do full credit to each side.

Where there is sorrow there is holy ground.

Oscar Wilde

We begin to be able to see how our past may be influencing our present in ways we want to change. We learn to use our overreactions to current life circumstances as indicators of where we have unfinished business from our pasts. If, for example, we find ourselves repeatedly getting into the same type of painful relationship, or being hurt regularly in the same way, or choosing friends or partners who treat us in ways that feel bad, we know we have unfinished business negatively impacting our current lives. That shows we need to go back to the source, the original situation or relationship that made us feel the same way that we feel in these current negative life patterns, in order to feel and see the original wound.

When we are traumatized, our response is fight, flight or freeze. Any of these responses help us to get through a traumatic situation by putting our feelings on hold so we can function. But now we need to go back and revisit the traumatic situation in order to feel it, process the unfelt feelings in context and come to understand them. While we are unconscious of or denying buried pain, anger and resentment, unconsciously we may choose situations and people to allow those feelings to come to the surface and be felt. It is our psyche's attempt to heal that pain.

Man is born child, his power is the power of growth.

Rabindranath Tagore

This is what projection is all about. We project onto others the feelings that we disown in ourselves and see these feelings as being exclusively about that present situation, not the past. But when we begin to grant our painful feelings and work them through, we don't need to use our present lives as outlets or repositories for the feelings. Though the process of making them conscious in order to move through them toward forgiveness and soul awareness is painful, it is ultimately faster and less destructive than denying them.

❦

Every real object must cease to be what it seemed,
and none could ever be what the whole soul desired.

George Santayana

STAGE THREE

ACCEPTANCE/LETTING GO

He that is discontented in one place
will seldom be happy in another.

Aesop

In the stage of acceptance, we *come to terms* either with what happened or with what never had a chance to happen. We realize that life isn't necessarily fair and that we are only continuing to hurt ourselves by holding onto resentment. We understand that in abusive situations, ultimately everyone is victimized to a greater or lesser extent and that the positions of the victim and the abuser are each opposite ends of a sick dynamic. When we accept what happened, it ceases to control our lives. It loses influence over us when we let go of the need to reenact the trauma incessantly in order to gain mastery over it, or in order to see, feel and understand it.

When we stop shaking our fists at the heavens, we free our

energies for perceptive living in the present. By separating past and present, we see that what happened just *happened*. It was not necessarily anyone's fault, including ours. Probably it was not *aimed* at us; it's possible that almost any other person standing on that spot at that moment would have received the same treatment—we were not the cause.

Along with this recognition comes the beginning of self-forgiveness. Getting squared away with the self, living with one's full humanity and seeing the self with compassion is an act of courage and humility. When we can do this, we become seasoned people for whom life does not need to prove itself repeatedly to be valued and savored, people who can enjoy feeling good without sabotaging that good for fear of losing it. We understand that it will be lost and found and lost again because that is the nature of life.

When we reach this point, we need to learn to allow ourselves to enjoy life, to let life feel good, to let it work out. This can be so anxiety provoking that we may even create problems to sabotage our happiness rather than accept and enjoy it. The abandonment anxiety that is aroused in a person who has endured deep loss can actually keep them from being able to live comfortably with good feeling. They sabotage what could be good because unconsciously they fear that if they let themselves get attached to it, trust it and let it feel good, they will not survive losing it again. Releasing the past and taking a leap of faith into the present is an important part of this stage, one that provides an opportunity to become philosophical and spiritual. It is an opportunity to learn the spiritual lesson that everything in life is temporary, life is change. In fact, clinging to situations or people creates instability and unhappiness. It's a paradox: we try to keep in our lives all that we love and need so we can feel stable, but true stability comes from our ability to live with constant flux. It is when we cannot tolerate the fluctuation that

A man who doesn't trust himself can never really trust anyone else.

Cardinal De Retz

we do things that create havoc in our lives. When the darts and arrows that are part of being human and alive are too much for us, we run to escape the perpetual low level of anxiety and pain that is part of living. It is what we run and escape into that creates a loss of self, that variety of "isms" that steal our souls.

When we accept that life offers no guarantees and that change is the only constant, we can live more easily with the anxiety that life engenders. Recognition and acceptance, not acquisition of a particular situation or person, ultimately will bring inner peace and contentment, because they enable us to let go

What loneliness is more lonely than mistrust.

George Eliot

of the fallacy that we will ever get it right once and for all. There is no once and for all; there is only now, today, the here-and-now. The house of soul is no house at all; it is simply the present, full of paradox, contradiction and unity through apparent disunity.

❦

The habit of looking for beauty in everything makes us notice the shortcomings of things; our sense, hungry for complete satisfaction, misses the perfection it demands.

George Santayana

STAGE FOUR

COMPASSION/FORGIVENESS

We must develop and maintain the capacity to forgive. He who is devoid of the power to forgive is devoid of the power to love. There is some good in the worst of us and some evil in the best of us. When we discover this, we are less prone to hate our enemies.

Dr. Martin Luther King, Jr.

In this stage, we develop the ability to reverse roles psychologically with the person with whom we have been having a problem, to feel as they might feel and see as they might see. This type of role reversal means that we can leave the self temporarily, look through another's eyes and then return to the self again. It is different from losing the self in another. It paves the way for genuine connection rather than connection through enmeshment. When we maintain a relationship with another person by sacrificing our own

The offender never pardons.

George Herbert

autonomy or a piece of ourselves, we are weakening our position rather than strengthening it. Role reversal is a psychically strong position because we can see both sides of the argument and hold them both in a compassionate light. It is not moti-

And all throughout eternity, I forgive you and you forgive me.

William Butler Yeats

vated by a wish to placate or smooth over; rather, it is motivated by a love of self and recognition of the self of another. The feeling beneath it is, "If I love myself, it is in my own best interest to be willing to see and to know all sides because ultimately it will free me." It is a step toward wisdom and maturity.

Along with this comes the ability to see the big picture, to step back from an isolated dynamic and take in the larger system. In this light, people's actions become more understandable and situations are less personalized. We learn not to take dysfunctional behavior so personally, understanding that after all we were not, nor *could* we have been, the whole cause, and we see that the same is true for the other person. We come to the awareness that most people do the best that they can with what they have to work with. In other words, if they had *known* better, they would have *done* better. Most people do not set out to

But life is hard for the man who quietly undertakes the way of perfection.

Buddha

be destructive; they are generally caught up in preserving their own defenses because they lack the ego strength to let them go. They or we were probably caught up in trying to survive using the tools we had. Though it is not remarkable or praiseworthy, it is less reprehensible than we may have thought. Compassion allows us to be present but not entangled, aware but not overly reactive. This position allows more of soul to express itself.

This is a stage at which we can begin to spin straw into gold, to use the trials and traumas of life to bring us closer to both our human and god-like natures. When we can begin to find meaning and purpose in suffering, to use it to deepen our relationship with life and self, we are living in the presence of soul. Forgiveness at this stage is a by-product rather than a goal. It is a spontaneous outcome of having come to understand. It is an outgrowth of growth, the blossom of a plant, something that is fragrant, elegant and alive, but with its roots in the soil of the unconscious. It is not independent, but part of the system; part of a life-giving process. When the clouds of doubt, the tears of pain, the storm of anger and rage are past, forgiveness is there, like a soft breeze on a summer afternoon that seems to come from nowhere and everywhere, from above and below, from within and without.

To err is human, to forgive divine.

Alexander Pope

This is why forgiveness cannot be an act of will and cannot be false. However long the process takes, whether it takes seconds or years, forgiveness is an act embodied by a whole personality, which is part of the larger body of the psyche. It is at once fully human and fully divine.

❦

Forgiveness is an interesting word. It does imply a giving—a giving in or giving up. The most common cause of depression is when a person is caught between the need to give up something and their will to hold on to it or their anger at having to give it up.

M. Scott Peck, M.D.

BONDING WITH THE SOUL

ANGER AND HURT

Reflection: Think of a circumstance in a relationship, either intimate or professional, that tends to repeat itself over and over again in your life and in which you end up feeling hurt or angry.

🍃 Notice if there is any pattern to the situation.

🍃 Does the pattern repeat itself?

🍃 How do you behave?

🍃 Do you get angry when you feel hurt?

🍃 Do you cry when you are angry?

🍃 Do you act as if you are angry at the other person, but secretly feel self-blame and self-doubt?

Journal: Just for the sake of exercise, write out all the angry feelings that you have felt toward a particular person, but never expressed to that person. For example, "I am angry at you because you . . . ," etc. Give your feelings full vent. As you read what you wrote, ask yourself:

🍃 Are these unexpressed feelings toward someone from your past being vented onto people in your life today, or possibly onto yourself?

🍃 If you are venting them onto yourself, how do you do that?

🍃 If you are venting them onto others, is it possible that you wait for an excuse to let go of built-up tension from unresolved past issues?

Journal: In this journal entry, consider a different way that pent-up feelings from a past situation may be causing you to behave toward others in a way that is not consistent with the real you. Writing in the first person, write a monologue from that person you are trying to hide inside yourself, the one you don't want anyone to see. For example: "I am Julie and I am small and frightened. Because I'm scared, I act certain ways and I scare people so they don't want to be with me." When you're finished, read over your monologue. It will help you to understand better how a past painful situation might have made you feel about yourself, because you feared what someone else felt about you.

BONDING WITH THE SOUL

SEPARATING THE PAST FROM THE PRESENT

Reflection: Allow yourself to relax in a place where you feel safe and comfortable. Let a painful situation that is present in your life come into your mind. Mentally experience yourself in that situation:

- ❧ How do you feel?

- ❧ Are you large or small?

- ❧ Are you powerful, dominated or just yourself?

- ❧ When did you feel like this before?

Journal: When you have identified a situation from your past in which you felt just as you feel in the present, let your mind bring the past situation and the people in it more clearly into your mind. Write a journal entry in the first person, writing as the child you were. For example: "My name is _____, I am seven years old. I am scared because I am hearing my parents fighting." When you're finished writing, reflect on what you wrote, whether it's paragraphs or pages. See if any feelings that are being triggered in your present-day situation are fueled by and made more intense by unresolved fears and feelings from your past.

BONDING WITH THE SOUL

LETTING GO

Reflection: Close your eyes, relax and get comfortable. Imagine that you have met a magic genie who has promised to grant you three wishes for how you would like your life to be, how you would like it to look, and who you would like to have in it. Really focus on each image so that you can see it clearly and sense the manifestation of the granting of your wish.

Journal: Choose one of your wishes and name it. Then write a few words, phrases or sentences that describe it. Next, write a few more words or phrases that describe how living with your granted wish feels. Write in the present tense, first person, as if it were actually happening. Now ask yourself:

ɬ When have you felt this way before?

ɬ How did things work out for you?

ɬ What are your fears about allowing yourself to feel like this again?

ɬ Where do you need to take a leap of faith?

BONDING WITH THE SOUL

CREATING CLOSURE

Reflection: Choose any stage of forgiveness that you feel drawn to. Read through the section, allow whatever thoughts and feelings that come to mind through reading to become conscious. Close your eyes and let the thoughts and feelings come into focus. If there is a person involved, let the person come to mind as well as the situation. Really be present to what is in your mind and experience it as fully as possible.

Journal: Choose whatever suggestion from the following that fits for you:

🖎 Write, but don't mail, a letter to a person saying what you need to say to bring closure to your thoughts and feelings.

🖎 Write a journal entry related to what is coming up for you.

🖎 Write a letter that you wish you had received. For example, a letter that you would like to have or feel you deserve from someone asking you for your forgiveness.

🖎 Reverse roles with the other person and write a journal entry as *that person*. For example, my name is so-and-so (other person's name) and I feel, etc.

6
Healing the Wounded Self

TRAUMA AND THE SOUL

Nothing in life is to be feared.
It is only to be understood.

Marie Curie

When we are confronted with a situation that is too frightening, painful or overwhelming to endure, we may react in one of three ways: fight, flight or freeze. When we do any one of these things, we do not experience the event fully and it gets stored in our brain in an unresolved state, without the closure that comes from experiencing a situation fully. This experience, unintegrated psychologically and emotionally, can become a wound that never heals, a live wire disconnected from the system.

Fight, flight and freeze are all attempts to leave the self, emotional responses that keep us from experiencing what is happening in the moment. They are natural responses to trauma. When we do not process and live through experience, however, it lives in us in an unfinished, open-ended state and becomes an emotional time bomb waiting to be tripped so it can finally go off to be seen and felt. Our unconscious actually may look for and even create circumstances to help us finish this unresolved aspect of ourselves. Events that let us speak the words we were never able to say, to touch, to hold, to push away, to cry, to yell, to give voice to what we have held so long in uncomfortable silence, hidden in the shadows of ourselves, tucked away where we thought it could not be seen, even by us. But these traumatized aspects of ourselves are pieces of our soul, frozen in silence, denied expression, told by another part of ourselves not to be.

The task of healing, then, is to bring these pieces of suspended self out into the arena of the living and breathe life back into them, to find understanding and meaning. To use them as grist for the mill, fertilizer for the growth of self, to transform pain into life learning and allow it to give us a fuller, richer, more expanded self able to experience soul.

Healing this kind of emotional trauma involves bringing the experience to a conscious level where we can feel and reexperience it; then we can fit all the missing pieces into context. We can gather the missing pieces of the puzzle of the self and see finally how it all fits together and we can sort out the distorted conclusions we have come to, conclusions that we have accepted as unalterable truth. Attempts we made to rationalize and explain irrational behavior can be seen for what they were. Finding some sort of meaning or potential for growth in the working through of the traumatic experience is a part of the healing process and the positive resolution and reintegration of the trauma into the self.

As Van der Kolk says, "Sudden, terrifying experiences which explode one's sense of predictability can have profound short-term and long-term effects on one's subsequent ways of dealing with emotions." The helplessness and rage which usually accompany these experiences may radically change a person's self-concept and interfere with the view that life is basically safe and predictable, a precondition for normal functioning. People seem to be psychologically incapable of accepting random, meaningless destruction and will search for any explanation to make meaning out of a catastrophe, including blaming themselves or their loved ones. Helplessness asks for a culprit. This may be either turned against the self for having been unable to prevent the inevitable, or against others. Because the effects of trauma are so detrimental to the development of a positive self-concept and feeling of trust in life, whether the trauma consisted of a terrifying event or long-term abuse or neglect at some time, it will need to be worked through. Distorted

> *The man who regards his own life and that of his fellow creatures as meaningless is not merely unfortunate but almost disqualified for life.*
>
> Albert Einstein

self concepts that we carry with us throughout our life can be the aftermath of trauma. A child who felt ignored, whose needs went unattended to, may be unable to put herself forward in a proactive, self-affirming way or may resent someone who can. Or she may be constantly chasing after recognition that never feels like enough. This can be seen as her attempt to work through the pain of not being seen and restoring herself to a feeling of wholeness. Resolving, surviving and mastering trauma even in retrospect can be very strengthening and broadening to the self and can free it from internal stress and pressure that keeps the self-system from feeling relaxed and present in the moment.

Experience, which destroys innocence,
also leads one back to it.

James Baldwin

BECOMING AWARE OF REPEATING PATTERNS

It's déjà vu all over again.

Yogi Berra

Our memory patterns are like frozen images stored in us. When an event feels good, we feel it and release it. When it hurts, we often defend against the pain by denying the full extent of it, and we repress it. Though consciously we are unaware of it, unconsciously it becomes a force to reckon with and finds its way to the surface of our lives in a variety of masked forms. Less and less of ourselves becomes available to us as we use our unconscious as a hiding place rather than a processing place. The more we are locked into our automatic patterns, the less awake and aware we are, and the less we are in communication with soul.

When we come to identify the patterns that we repeat over and over again or the experiences that we seem to draw into our lives repeatedly, even though we don't necessarily want them to be there, we learn which emotional issues are still unresolved. Repeating the same painful behaviors over and over again is the psyche's attempt to heal itself from a wound or trauma that has not become fully conscious.

Understanding *how* we experienced certain life events gives us greater knowledge of ourselves and more detachment from our self-destructive patterns, which in turn allows us to lead our lives with more conscious awareness. When we refuse to remember the pain of early experiences, refuse to sit with it and feel it, we may project that pain onto others and make it about them. Rather than resolve the issue, we will compound it.

What we can do is try to determine what pattern of relating or situation we are repeating, and of what earlier experience it reminds us. When we can contact and trace back through memory and association the earlier experience that was painful or traumatizing, we can make the connection between the repetition of the pattern in our lives and that early experience. When we can see the pattern repetition as an attempt to recreate that situation from early in life so that we can experience it without feeling traumatized by it, we can begin to loosen the pattern's grip.

❦

Respect the past in the full measure of its deserts,
but do not make the mistake of confusing it with the present,
nor seek it in the ideals of the future.

Jose Ingenieros

PROCESSING FEELINGS

Recent scientific findings have led the search for heart health into a new domain: that of the spirit. An increasing number of cardiologists, mind-body therapists, and psychologists are counseling heart patients and others at risk for heart disease to harness spiritual power in the prevention and treatment of heart disease. In some medical circles, prescriptions for cholesterol-lowering drugs, beta-blockers, angioplasties, and bypass operations are no longer automatic. The new prescriptions include prayer, practicing forgiveness, going to church or temple, and surrendering to a divine authority.

These developments beg the question: Is the heart merely a pump supported by an adequate flow of oxygenated blood and a steady supply of nutrients? Or is this fist-sized muscular organ the "seat of the soul," requiring nourishment on a spiritual level? If it is both, then what is the relationship between the physical and the metaphorical heart?

—Henry Dreher

As humans we have feelings about virtually everything we encounter. These feelings or emotions simply *are.* Often, however, we think we shouldn't feel a certain way. When we regard certain feelings as "good" and others as "bad," we erect an inner barrier that disallows us to experience them and prevents us from moving through them easily and integrating them.

> **Resistance is the first step to change.**
>
> Louise Hay

The concept of ordinary soul includes accepting ordinary feelings. When we try to run away or deny them, we may act them out in destructive ways. Sitting with our emotions and simply experiencing them allows them to be released and integrated into the energy of the self. When we see that our emotions are energy, we feel less need to label them in order to understand them because their meaning becomes clear as we allow ourselves to feel them. But when we label certain emotions bad, we tend to disown them, thinking that by disowning them they will disappear. Quite the contrary; the very process of disowning them increases their power. It inhibits the experience of an easy, accepting emotional flow from person to person.

Rather than run from certain emotions, let's try encountering them differently. When a particular emotion makes us feel panicky and we want to run from it or shut it off, rather than disavowing the feeling, let's accept that we feel it, explore it, examine it from different perspectives. The philosopher J. Krishnamurti suggested that emotions have their own life cycle, like a flower. If we allow them to bloom within us, come into their full color and scent, and slowly wilt, the energy contained in them will also follow this pattern and they will be moved through and reintegrated within us. In this way our emotions offer us an opportunity to grow and become intimate with our inner selves. When we do not run from our feelings out of fear and panic, we stay in tune with our selves.

❦

Seeing's believing,
but feeling's the truth.

Thomas Fuller

SUFFERING

Suffering is the sole origin of consciousness.

Fyodor Dostoyevski

Like fire, suffering has the power to reshape and redefine. When we run from pain, we avoid something that can help us to pass through darkness into light, through hurt into awakening, through pain into compassion. When we run from suffering, we run from ourselves and an opportunity for soul growth. It can be through our woundedness that our inner vision opens. It is through our suffering that we develop knowledge of our own and others' humanity. As Emily Dickinson said, "The *wounded* Deer leaps highest."

Suffering is to the heart and soul as tears are to the eyes, cleansing and expelling toxicity from the inner system. When we do not allow ourselves to feel appropriate pain, we move into a sort of non-experience. We watch life rather than live it; we look but never get too close.

There is a vast difference between observing or witnessing our own inner process and staring at it from a position of emotional shutdown. When we shut down our sentient selves, it is as if we are sitting down to a banquet we cannot taste—we eat the food but do not experience any flavor. When we refuse to suffer, we shut down the parts of ourselves that give life meaning and depth, that make one day different from the other, one experience different from the next, one person separate from the rest.

Our feelings provide information about our personal preferences. Without this information we lose touch with ourselves and cannot tell the difference between one feeling and another, one person and another. Without feeling, says Edna St. Vincent Millay, our "souls are flat."

The human brain grows with use, new information creates brain growth and alters cell assemblies or particular constellations of memories. In order to grow, we must struggle. Children need to struggle through each stage of development, to move out of one skin and into another, to solve new life equations, to risk, to succeed, to fail and to continue. Part of struggling is working through previous stages into new ones, changing thoughts and behavior patterns with new energy, continually shaping and reshaping the self.

Finding meaning and new and deeper understanding of life and self as a result of working through pain is one of the most important tasks of life. This is how we spin gold out of straw.

❦

Although the world is full of suffering, it is also full of the overcoming of it.

Helen Keller

ANGER

*Anger is often more hurtful
than the injury which caused it.*

English saying

Anger is not bad, it is what we *do* with it that gets us into trouble. Above all, we need to *feel* our anger. While in the heat of the moment we may think it is our right to dump our anger on those around us, this can be an attempt *not to feel it.* Worse, although we get rid of the feeling, we don't learn anything from it.

Anger can tell us important information about our self. When anger is appropriate—when it is not an attempt to dump, control or purge our feelings at someone else's expense—it tells us where our boundaries are, what just hurt, what felt invasive or who did not respect who we are. We need this information to keep ourselves safe and to know what works for us and what doesn't. Our anger is telling us that something didn't feel right and we need to examine it to see what our reaction is about. In this case, all we need to do is *tolerate our anger,* experience it and investigate what is going on for us, so that we can respond better next time to take care of ourselves.

Inappropriate anger is generally a larger and more intense reaction than the situation merits. When it occurs, it is wise to check with the self to see if there is an historical component; is all of this anger really only about the situation at hand, or is a deeper anger being triggered that is part of our excess baggage from the past?

If the anger is being triggered by current circumstances but fueled by unresolved past hurt and pain, you have an opportunity for self-cleansing and growth. Rather than curse the situation or person who is bringing up this feeling, ask yourself, "Am I really angry at this person, or at someone from my past with whom I have unresolved issues? Am I really angry at this situation, or does it put me in touch with something that happened in the past about which I feel anxious and incomplete?" It is useful then to allow into consciousness the person or situation from the past that is being warmed up to surface, in order to see what really is going on and to make a connection between the present and the past circumstance.

The goal is to *separate the past from the present* and free the self of its need to project anger inappropriately to get rid of it. Ultimately, feeling the anger and processing it will be much more useful and satisfying than dumping it irrationally. It will reintegrate the previous painful experience with new insight and understanding, taking steps toward freeing the self of the unfinished business.

※

The hot sun melts the snows; when anger comes, wisdom goes.

Hindu proverb

RETRIBUTION

A man that studieth revenge keeps his own wounds green,
which otherwise would heal and do well.

Francis Bacon

Each of us comes to the point on our path to soulfulness when we are faced with letting go of old resentment and hurt. Desire for retribution is one of the major blocks to moving beyond pain. We want to make the person who hurt us suffer as we feel they made us suffer. Unfortunately, though, the hatred and resentment that we carry in our hearts for the other person is carried just there, in *our* hearts. If we could truly put it on the other person without having to carry it within us, our retribution would be complete. But we can't;

we are hurting ourselves. In fact, we are twice hurt, initially when they hurt us, and now by carrying anger and rage within our very being. By doing so, we have given them tremendous power over us.

We are locked in a bind. We do not get the justice and satisfaction that we feel we so richly deserve, while at the same time we are unable to extricate ourselves from the terrible feelings we carry inside. We are free only when we have our own feelings back in a true sense: that is, we take hold of ourselves—our inner nature and soul force—once again, rather than let ourselves dissipate in old grudges and held resentment.

All the wisdom in the world cannot put in one's heart the love one yearned for as a small child. Consider, for instance, Lydia, whose father was a hurtful and abusive alcoholic. Although her mother did not overtly abuse or punish her, she did little to protect her, and she ignored her profoundly. Lydia felt, as psychiatrist John Bowlby, M.D., puts it, "alone in the presence of the mother."

Lydia experienced her mother's disinterest as a denial of her very self. As a youngster she had no one to affirm her, to mirror her presence, and to call her forth out of her childhood silence. She was alone in the presence of the person she most desperately wished to be seen by, and nothing she could do or be or say could draw to her the love and attention, or earn the positive regard that she wanted so deeply.

For children to suffer this lack of regard makes them feel like they do not exist. It does not feel like an emotional issue, but rather a survival issue. How can they be worthy human beings that the world will someday love and accept if their own parents find them unacceptable?

Lydia is now a grown woman with a husband, a home and children of her own. She has done the inner work necessary not to pass on her mother's disinterest to her own children. Rather, she has loved them and nurtured them throughout their lives. Her mother is now at an age where she realizes some of what she has missed. Though she does not see the entirety of it, she has an inkling that she was not particularly present during the years of raising her children. She wishes now for Lydia's love and acceptance.

The dilemma that Lydia faces is that she now is being asked, by the very woman who withheld positive regard and love, to give freely those very things. The little girl who was hurt and forgotten, who still lives inside of Lydia, hears this request from her mother and screams out in anger, "No! Never! You hurt me too much. You didn't give it to me so I won't give it to you. Go away!" But Lydia herself is not fully comfortable with this position. Not because she doesn't understand why she wants to withhold love from her mother, but because no one really wants to send a parent to his or her grave with rancor in her heart. At least, most people do not.

Lydia is asked to give love from an empty place that her mother didn't fill. She is asked to give what she didn't get to the very person who didn't give it to her. Lydia is not superhuman. She knows what she would like to do but finds herself unable to do it. She knows the sense of liberation she would find in not feeling the need to trade insult for insult, to undermine and diminish her mother in the way that she felt undermined and diminished by her mother. She sees that spiritually, her feelings are an obstacle to her serenity and of feeling good about herself.

To move beyond a need for retribution is an act of surrender and selfless love. In a sense, it is a humble recognition of our basic humanity, acknowledgment of the powerlessness each of us has sometime during the course of our own lives, and even at times over our own behavior and personality. To move beyond retribution is a way of saying, as is expressed in the Jewish seder, "It is enough. What I got was enough." When we can do this, something inside us opens and we begin to fill from another source, a mysterious source, a source which we cannot see or touch but which has, nonetheless, a powerful presence within us. When we can fill up in this way, the hollow emptiness inside fills from within and what comes to us from outside, whether it be good or bad, interested or indifferent, has less power to define us and hold us in its thrall.

When we let go of the need to be wrong or right, we feel an inner freedom that we do not allow ourselves when we are busy categorizing, labeling and tracing the dimensions of interactions, situations and people. We accept that we don't have all the answers and that there may be aspects of a reality that we do not fully understand or perceive. Then we can let go of the endless detective work required when we feel that we are somehow able to solve all things in our consciousness. When we allow ourselves to know that we cannot comprehend everything, that sometimes we need to surrender the controls because we have recognized that control is, after all, only the illusion of control, we are setting the wheels in motion for inner movement towards spirit.

ᕯ

You can't hold a man down without staying down with him.

Booker T. Washington

SELFISHNESS, NARCISSISM AND SELF-REALIZATION

I hate the philosopher who is not wise for himself.

Euripides

Being honest with ourselves is one of the main stepping stones along the path to individuation. When we resist understanding and accepting what is really true for us, our points of self-reference will not be useful because they will not be founded on our personal truths. Our path toward self-understanding and self-realization is our path toward soul. It is the work of a lifetime. Each time we expose a new layer to the light of conscious scrutiny we come to know, to cleanse, to reorganize and reintegrate that layer into ourselves. Then we can begin to work on the next layer.

This type of self-absorption is the opposite of selfishness.

Selfishness is an effort to collect experiences, people, objects and so on in an attempt to gather a *self*. In reality, it is only an exercise in gathering a non-self because the self is not something we can grab from outside and stuff into us. Rather, self-understanding, soul-knowledge is a process of unfolding from within, shedding false identities, and allowing an inner self to become increasingly evident in our psyches and in our lives.

Nor is the process of soul-knowledge narcissism. The kind of self-absorption experienced by narcissists comes from a lack of self. Because narcissists lack a basic self, they make the people close to them, as well as their possessions and activities, extensions of themselves. Perhaps they feel that if they can get enough of what is around them claimed as self, they will find self somewhere along the way, or at least pieces of self. Narcissists operate from a place of inner woundedness and emptiness that they have never been able to own. That is part of why it is so painful to have close relationships with narcissistic people. The feeling of emptiness began so early in life that they don't know they are empty. All they know is that they have an indistinct, pervasive feeling of need so overwhelming that they dare not feel it. Consequently, they seek to indenture those around them and incorporate them into their inner world in an attempt to fill their emptiness. They give with one hand and take with the other. People in their presence rarely feel seen as individuals or understood for themselves because narcissistic people do not have that understanding to give them. Indeed, they hardly understand themselves.

Seeking individuation and soul realization is not selfishness. The search includes recognition that at the deepest level one's self is connected with the self of others. Thus, doing what is best spiritually for the self often means doing something ultimately of benefit for others.

When we learn to respond to the needs of the higher self rather than the lower self, our vision of self alters. We gain a new perspective on ourselves and the world, and we come to see that in treating others well, we are treating ourselves well, because it is impossible to separate what is connected on the fundamental level of energy. The Golden Rule, "Do unto others as you would have others do unto you," is a path toward sane and happy living. In a world that is connected on the particle or energy level, all actions, whether toward self or others, are also connected fundamentally. Self-realization or soul-realization, then, is an antidote to narcissism in our world today, which tends to manipulate the outside in order to fill up the inside.

Self-realization is a step our culture can take in order not to become narcissistically self-absorbed in the process of accumulating more. In self-realization we make a decision to *drop* within, where we see the table prepared for us.

᭡

Thus, self-realization is not a fashionable
experiment but the highest task an individual can
undertake. For himself, it means the possibility of
an anchor in what is indestructible and
imperishable, in the primordial nature of the
objective psyche. By self-realization he returns to
the eternal stream in which birth and death are only
stations of passage and the meaning of life no
longer resides in the ego. Towards others it raises
up within him the tolerance and kindness that is
only possible in those who have explored and
consciously experienced their own darkest depths.
Toward the collectivity, its special value is that
it can offer society a fully responsible individual
who knows the obligation of the particular to the
general from his own most personal experience, the
experience of his own psychic brutality.

J. Jacobi

BONDING WITH THE SOUL

PAINFUL MOMENTS

Reflection: Not only traumatic incidents cause problems, but our many reactions to painful moments or periods of time can be experienced as traumatic and can create complications later. For example, the trauma of war and gunfire may be an initial trauma, but the reverberations may be fear of loud noises, fear of going out at night, fear of new or strange places, fear of joining a crowd for a group endeavor, fear of entering any situation that may hold surprises, etc.

Allow to surface in your mind a traumatic situation where there was a singular event or a period in your life where you sustained serious stress: for example, living with an alcoholic or the aftereffects of a car accident. Allow the feelings that you were not able to experience then to surface now to the extent that feels manageable to you.

Journal: In the center of the page, describe in brief phrases the situation that has come into your mind. Around this description use feeling words to describe how this situation made you feel. After you have finished, ask yourself how the unresolved feelings stemming from these early painful events get in the way of your living comfortably today.

BONDING WITH THE SOUL

PROCESSING FEELINGS

Reflection: Allow to rise into your consciousness a situation that makes you feel anxious. Let the full situation come into view. See the people. Feel the place or circumstance. Sense the environment where it takes place.

Journal: In the center of the page, draw a circle. Inside the circle, write the name of the situation or person or people you are thinking about. Now all around the circle, write feeling words that describe the way you experience this situation. Allow yourself really to feel each and every feeling that you have written down, one at a time. Do not judge them or yourself as good or bad; simply have the feelings you have. Do you notice that your attitudes shift in any way when you do not deny yourself your own feelings, but just allow them to be?

7
Hiding from the Self

THE DISOWNED SELF

There is simply no more consequential step to be taken than the abandonment of the real self. . . . The energies driving toward self-realization are shifted to the aim of actualizing the idealized self.

Karen Horney

When we lose contact with our inner self, we may fill that empty place by creating an *idealized self,* an image of the person we want the world to see when they look at us. The heavier the reliance on our idealized self, the more out of touch we become with our inner self. Rather than put energy toward actualizing the real self, the self that connects with soul, we put our energy and attention toward an illusion. The more we try to blow life into a hollow shell, the less authentically we are able to live. This syndrome of heavy reliance on an idealized self is strengthened in families that model perfection and have personal values that demand that the family appear perfect. When human foibles and inadequacies must be hidden to serve an idealized image, the energy that might have gone into building a soul and a relationship with self is retracked into building a proper image.

It takes all our energy to maintain an idealized image. If we allowed ourselves to experience a full range of feelings, we would have to adjust our idealized image to reality rather than to the ideal. And so we choose not to feel those feelings that threaten, challenge or undermine our idealized image of self. Sometimes we take those feelings, those parts of ourselves that we find repugnant, and we cast them into our internal darkness. There they continue to live and grow in the shadow self, the self we attempt to deny.

Most of us form idealized selves to cope with overwhelming, conflicting, painful or out-of-control feelings, or feelings that conflict with our image of ourselves. If we deny these feelings in ourselves, we may project them onto someone else. Then, when we observe the feeling in the other person, we forget it was ours to begin with.

Sadly, projecting our feelings muddies the waters of relationships. If, for example, I cannot accept that I am jealous of other people and have competitive feelings toward them, I may project those feelings onto others by seeing them as jealous and competitive and myself as the object of their jealousy. I can never really get to the bottom of the situation because I cannot get to the bottom of my own feelings. Pieces of the puzzle are missing, and the biggest piece is me.

This dynamic occurs all too often in child-rearing. Parents who are uncomfortable with their own feelings project the feelings onto the children, who aren't in a position to refute them.

Another form this dynamic can take is that of *projective identification*. In projective identification, an aspect of the self that we don't want to acknowledge is placed, not in the working model of the self, but in that of another to whom the self is closely related. The other is then seen as having a bad attitude. Instead of distancing the other person, we may provoke the other person into hostile behavior, thus creating a basis for the projection.

The family arena is a fertile ground for the dynamics of projection and projective identification. Because identities overlap in families and people share the same emotional atmosphere, it can be hard to know who is feeling what. In a family we get to know each other's buttons so well that we can push them almost effortlessly. Once we have pushed the right button and caused a person to feel a particular way, the projective identification has taken place. It is easier for some people to provoke anger in another person rather to know they carry anger within themselves.

The remedy, as always, is to bring the focus back to oneself and to sit with an open and willing attitude, ready to know one's own inner makeup. The first step on the road back to self is to know that no matter how long you have denied your true self, it can still be accessed. If you are willing simply to sit with your self and listen, you will hear the small voice of your soul calling you back home.

❧

Our shadow will follow us.

Tamil

DEFENSES

The teeth are smiling but is the heart?

Congolese proverb

When thoughts, feelings or emotions are painful or disturbing, we may try to get rid of them through denial, suppression and repression, to mask them from ourselves.

In *denial*, we rewrite painful or threatening experiences to make them of less concern. For instance, Robert and Susan were out for dinner with friends. Robert had a few too many drinks, his jokes got a little raucous, his humor a little borderline, and when he danced with Fred's wife, he held her in a way that made her uncomfortable. Susan noticed Fred glancing toward his wife. Rather than experience her own discomfort at Robert's behavior, however, Susan wrote the situation: Robert is so handsome, all women just naturally flirt with him and Fred is jealous. Robert's humor, though off-color, is actually quite daring; he says things that are on everybody's minds but nobody will say. In this way, Susan explains away her own discomfort and the discomfort that she senses around her.

Denial is subtle and can be hard to identify, particularly when we become increasingly talented rewriters of feelings. A good denier can be hard to keep up with and can make others feel out of step with reality. The purpose of denying feelings is to reduce anxiety and then rewrite the situation into an acceptable one because we get uncomfortable when someone we depend on for love and security is unreliable or falling apart. If our lives might be in trouble, denial is easier.

The last thing people in denial want to hear is the truth that they fear is lurking beneath the rewrite. When confronted with it, we will try to make the person feel wrong or bad for bringing it up. We may even need to rewrite the person's reasons for bringing it up. For example, if Fred mentions his discomfort with Robert's behavior toward his wife, Susan will simply tell herself that Fred is insecure seeing his wife get attention from another man. Susan may even congratulate herself for her apparent equanimity in the face of her husband's obvious flirting with another woman. As we see here, denial has an insidious quality that can be very hard to detach from the truth of the situation.

In *suppression,* however, thoughts that we find bothersome are consciously relegated to another place in the mind. We make the decision not to dwell on them. Suppression, in fact, has at times been thought to be the right way to handle painful situations. Though suppression can be an effective coping skill and can reduce stress successfully, if used too often it can be used against itself. It is healthy and necessary to know when to let go of a negative thought and when it becomes self-defeating to go over it constantly, reworking it, seeking more and more from it. However, if we begin to avoid all hurtful thoughts and see it as a strength not to "dwell on the negative," to "keep a stiff upper lip," it can create tension within the personality. Tension builds into stress and stress seeks relief. If we suppress too much, it may get released inappropriately or we may reach for a stress-relieving substance or activity.

It is probably more useful simply to allow the thought and not feel a need to react to it one way or another. With some level of detachment, we can recognize the thought as arising from our own minds, appropriate to our own thinking process or history, but not become so identified with the thought that it must be dealt with harshly. If anxiety is associated with the thought, it is probably more useful in the long run just to feel it in the moment, allow it to be and allow it to expend its own energy. If we do not interfere with it by trying to get rid of it or manipulating it, chances are this entire process will not take more than a few minutes. On the other hand, if it gets suppressed over and over and over, it becomes a tangled mass that has to be undone later.

Repression is motivated selective forgetting that relieves us from having to remember something that makes us uncomfortable. The repressed material is stored in the unconscious and can return unbidden. Freud postulated two types of repression. The first is "primal repression," involving denying entry into consciousness of threatening material. In this type of repression, thoughts are relegated to the unconscious *before we ever becomes aware of them,* so it appears as though we never perceived the material. The second type is "repression proper," or after expulsion. This involves assignment of material to the unconscious after the material has been consciously recognized.

A client in one of my therapy groups explained that she had come into a group situation because she needed to learn how to connect with people. She felt that she built walls around herself and would not let others get past them to know what she called the real her. She described her relationship with her ex-husband as functional enough to raise their children together, but they had never really gotten to know one another. Now, in group, she felt in a bind. On one hand she could not stand the intimate feelings that she experienced in group therapy, and on the other she wanted to fix the problem. She was uncomfortable and anxious and vacillated between wanting to bawl out group members for what she perceived to be their various inadequacies, and feeling that it was up to her to take care of them and make them feel comfortable.

One of the purposes of group therapy is to learn how to resolve our struggle with uncomfortable feelings. Unfortunately, this woman couldn't stop swinging between her two coping techniques. In group, whenever her feelings got too intense for her, she took care of others, asking how they felt, what was wrong, and offering advice and solutions. It was not particularly comfortable for other group members who wanted to explore their own feelings without intrusion. Her behavior served to shut them down, just as it shut down her own rapidly rising anxiety. When repressed material came too close to the surface, she leapt toward others to counsel and caretake in an attempt to flee from her own repressed feelings.

Unless repressed material can be made conscious, it will continue to dictate our behavior by causing us to avoid or anesthetize the feared feelings. Interestingly, people who finally do feel the repressed feeling generally experience a great sense of relief. The feelings that they so feared would overwhelm them actually were less threatening than when they were repressed. When repression begins in childhood, a time when most situations really are out of our control, repression can seem to be the best way to cope with feelings we can't handle. When we experience these feelings again as adults, something fundamental has changed. As adults we're no longer at the same risk and we are able to see that our feelings may have been a natural part of being a powerless child. In a therapeutic situation, the intensity of the feeling can be felt safely, released and reintegrated into the unconscious along with new understanding and awareness.

Intellectualization is a defense that is hard to identify because what is said *sounds* so good. Intellectualization also is an effective way to hide from the self. We feel that, if the reasons are good enough, the truth can be discarded, ignored or explained away. Eventually, being in the presence of intellectualizing becomes infuriating because we feel we will never get close to what is really going on. That's because the purpose of intellectualization is to keep people away from what's happening in the deep layers of a situation.

Another aspect of intellectualization is *rationalization*. Rationalization may be using a good reason, but not the *real* reason, for behavior. For example, Carol goes shopping to make herself feel better. She rationalizes that since she has the money that her husband works so hard for, she might as well enjoy spending a little of it. Actually, she's using shopping as a way to manage or chase away feelings of emptiness and a sense of being taken for granted by her spouse. She may rationalize that the children need new clothes for fall or that she absolutely needs items for the house. It's true, children do need clothes for fall and a house is always in need of attention, but her relationship to shopping goes deeper. Though her reasons make sense, she is using them as defenses against her real feelings of loneliness.

When we use intellectualization, rationalization or any of the other defenses to keep from feeling what we really feel, we close off parts of ourselves. Going shopping relieves the empty feeling only momentarily. Without spending the time and energy to investigate what is really going on, our thinking becomes a foggy mirror, while moving through the defenses cleans the mirror of self so we can gain a clear reflection.

You can only find truth with logic
if you have already found truth without it.

G. K. Chesterton

PERFECTIONISM

Any plan is bad that cannot be changed.

Italian proverb

Perfectionism is an enemy of soul growth. Jane, a sophisticated woman in her sixties, mother of three, stepmother of four, grandmother of eight and stepgrandmother of six, was going over her Christmas plans. She began to feel overwhelmed with the season's gift-buying, cooking and entertaining. Jane liked to do things perfectly, and Christmas was no different. Buying and wrapping the gifts, putting the food on the table, arranging the table decorations, adding the little Christmasy touches throughout the house, all had to meet a high standard for Jane to see them as worthy of the season. "You know me," she said. "If I can't do it perfectly, I'd rather not do it at all."

Jane's statement carried a shade of superiority, even smugness. Seeing herself as a perfectionist was, for her, seeing herself as somehow superior to other people. I thought of her grandchildren coming over for Christmas day and looking under the tree for their presents. I thought of her children who, though grown and married themselves, would think of gathering around a Christmas tree as part of the festivities, part of what they would like to share with their children. I don't think they would have noticed or cared if the tree was trimmed perfectly. In fact, the very tension created by the holiday having to go just right effectively drained much warmth and spontaneity from it. After all, perfect was only Jane's version of perfect, and for everyone to be tuned in to her version of it, so they could act appropriately and not displease her, was a preoccupying task. It took quantities of people's energy that could have been spent on relaxing and having a good time.

Being perfectionistic keeps us from having to accept that life's messiness will never be solved, it will never be perfect. Believing that a perfect situation or person is possible, is looking for utopia. Part of growing up, maturing and soulful living is giving up the illusion of perfection and accepting that life is what's happening right now, nothing more and nothing less. Having life go perfectly will not keep things from going wrong. Count on it. Up and down is the nature of living.

When we indenture ourselves to maintaining a perfect state, we create an impossible situation. Perfection is unachievable. It is an illusion against which we measure ourselves. How many relation-ships have been cast aside because they did not fulfill our ideas of what they *should be?* As long as we are lost in the illusion, we are not present in the here and now, and soul is in the present moment, not in the illusion. How much of our energies are wasted chasing after what might be or could have been? The task of soul is to learn to see perfection in things *as they are*, in *recognizing* perfection in what already is.

❧

A good garden may have some weeds.

Thomas Fuller

RAGE

Hell has three gates: lust, anger and greed.

Bhagavad Gita

The frightening, intense explosion we call rage may be made of many layers of withheld anger that were never felt, processed and understood, anger that had nowhere to go, no one who cared, no one who would listen. When anger is forced down, it acquires a life of its own. It is no longer about anything but itself.

When it is held in, rage causes problems on physical, emotional and spiritual levels. People hold onto rage because they are afraid of it. If they were not, it would not have become a problem. It would have come and gone, been felt, understood and integrated. Rage is anger that has not gone through this normal process but has stayed locked in the self. It needs to surface gradually, guided by cognition and memory, so we can see what we were angry about and why we couldn't express it or even allow ourselves to feel it.

When it is inappropriately released, rage has the power to destroy both spirit and self. It can murder the soul or become the irrational fuel to kill another person. Since rage usually accumulates over a long period of time, it is best released over time. It does not go away all at once, nor does it always surface to be worked through. When it does come, if it is a quiet or even a silent rage, it may not even be seen.

When, for instance, children are made to feel that their anger is bad and they are not allowed to feel and process it, they come to feel that *they* are bad, that something about them is ugly or wrong. It may be complicated further by parents who ask their children to deny justified anger, when they, themselves, are guilty of behaving in ways that cause that anger. This puts the child in an emotional bind of feeling anger toward the very person who is telling them to hide it or *not to feel it*.

Because sharing and resolution of the child's anger isn't possible, it turns inward and comes out in other ways. It may be acted out inappropriately on others, channeled into competition, or held within the self until it builds up and distorts thinking, perception and behavior in subtle ways. It may become sideways anger—criticism, sarcasm, whining, control or meanness.

Above all, anger needs to be felt so it can be talked through, understood and integrated, rather than acted out. In this way, it cleanses the self, and guards against fueling compulsion or self-destructiveness. It frees one to be more fully in the self, to inhabit one's own personality without trying to flee from it, which allows the soul to inhabit the self as well.

❦

It is easy to fly into a passion—anybody can do that. But to be angry with the right person to the right extent at the right time and with the right object in the right way, that is not easy, and it is not everyone who can do it.

Aristotle

DEPRESSION

Sorrow is to the soul what the worm is to the wood.

Turkish proverb

Depression can feel like a black cloud that descends over us without warning, blocking us from the light and leaving us utterly without hope. Although it seems to come out of nowhere, it may have several real sources. There is the depression that weighs heavily on body and spirit, the result of years of unfelt, unexpressed anger turned inward. There is the depression that comes from unfelt sadness, frozen tears that were held too long inside, waiting for a safe time and place to flow. There is also something that can feel like depression but is really despair. Paradoxically, this can be almost good news, because it means that we have reached bottom at last, and there is nowhere to go but up.

When we recover from depression, all the feelings that have been numbed in an attempt to get by, to look good, or to hide, will be warmed in the healing process. As the frozen self begins to melt, the anger courses through us like life returning to the body. It may seem inappropriate or out of control, but it is part of the healing, part of reconnecting with the self. Tears that welled in our eyes without falling now will at last be released. We can give voice to a wail that rocks us to the core.

The mass of men lead lives of quiet desperation.

Henry David Thoreau

People who come back from depression feel they are being reborn because they reexperience parts of themselves and feelings they forgot existed. Part of this rebirth is feeling all of our emotions, as if for the first time, and this can be both joyful and fearful, exhilarating and unsteadying. The road back from depression is rocky and full of emotion. But when our depression has lifted, we will be on speaking terms with parts of ourselves that we have not met for years.

❧

The great art of life is sensation,
to feel that we exist, even in pain.

Lord Byron

THE DYNAMICS OF SHAME

The more sinful and guilty a person tends to feel, the less chance there is that he will be
a happy, healthy law abiding citizen. He will become a compulsive wrongdoer.

Dr. Albert Ellis

Shame is quicksand on the path to soul. When shame holds us in its powerful grip, it is easy to sink into it and be consumed by it, losing perspective and reason, unable to break free. Unlike guilt, which generally is specific to a circumstance or situation, shame tends to be a more pervasive and debilitating attitude toward the self.

When shame feels unbearable, consciously or unconsciously we may try to get rid of it by passing it onto others, undermining them, criticizing them, being judgmental or cruel. Or we can pass on shame by running from the feeling, trying to lose ourselves in some activity. At its worst, shame can be fuel for abusive, compulsive and addictive behavior. The dynamics of intergenerational shame, or passing shame-based pain on through the generations, is caused by the need to avoid feeling shame, so we engender shame in someone else.

Do as the heavens have done, forget your evil; With them forgive yourself.

William Shakespeare

The remedy is to own and experience our shame, bringing it out into the light for a good look. What is it about? Where did it come from? Shame thrives in shadows. Once it is owned and shared in a safe environment, it begins to lose its power.

This old wisdom was practiced years ago when the church con-
fessional was not a closed box but an open discussion. When we
share those parts of ourselves about which we *Confession is good*
feel shame, we break our isolation, allow others *for the soul.*
to identify with us and identify with others as they Scottish proverb
share. We all carry shame to some degree. Sharing
it lightens the load and pulls it out of the secret undercurrents where
it might get passed along in silence, into the light of day where it can
dissipate and detoxify, leaving the emotional system free to breathe
and heal.

❦

I am content to follow to its source
Every moment in action or in thought;
Measure the lot; forgive myself the lot!
When such as I cast out remorse
So great a sweetness flows into the breast
We must laugh and we must sing,
We are blest by everything
Everything we look upon is blest.

W. B. Yeats

HARSH INNER VOICES

Life consists in what a man is thinking all day.

Ralph Waldo Emerson

Sometimes it is not the voices of others that have the power to
harm us as much as our own *inner voices* that echo in the chambers

of our hearts. It is worthwhile to stand back for a moment and listen to the way you talk to yourself. What do you say to yourself if you haven't done a good job, or you feel that you don't look good? If you've never taken the time to listen to those voices, you may be surprised at how harsh you are to yourself.

Where do these voices come from? Some of them are the internalized voices of our parents, other adults, siblings or early school friends. Others are the unspoken criticisms and implicit judgments that we feared the authority figures in our life were feeling toward us. Generally, if people feel good about themselves, they tend to feel good about those around them. People who regularly expressed negative feelings toward us probably were feeling that way about themselves. Finally, we took in their attitudes as our own self-concepts.

Are these inner voices truly ours? Do they have our best interests in mind? Do we really agree with what they are saying?

In our journey toward self-realization, we must learn to work with these destructive voices, identify them for what they are and not let them define and control us. We need to create and nurture a voice that does not undermine our progress through life, but encourages our positive growth toward real self-awareness.

❧

Change your thoughts and you change your world.

Norman Vincent Peale

BONDING WITH THE SOUL

Perfectionism

Reflection: Allow yourself to have a moment of self-honesty.

- How do you hurt yourself by judging yourself harshly for not living up to your expectations, your ideas of how you *should* be?

- What do you tell yourself or expect of yourself that leaves you feeling not good enough or as if you don't measure up?

Journal: Give a voice to the part of you that wants to be free and whole. Write a journal entry from or as the person inside of you whom you are judging or ignoring. Allow part of yourself to describe how it feels to hear these harsh, judgmental voices. Next, and also from this part of yourself, write between 10 and 20 things that you like about yourself. For example: "I am Judy and I have a wonderful laugh. I am Judy and I like the way I like people." Make your list as long as you like. You may share this list with a trusted person if you choose.

BONDING WITH THE SOUL

DEFENSES

Reflection: Allow yourself to reflect on situations in which you feel vulnerable, circumstances in which you feel shaky inside. Imagine that you had the magical ability to conjure up a shield.

- What could the shield do for you?

- What would this shield protect you from that you don't want to experience?

- What might the shield keep you from that you would like to experience but are afraid to?

Journal: If the shield could talk, what would it say? Write a journal entry *as the shield*. Write in the first person. "I am Jane's shield and I protect her from feeling pain when she gets too attached to a man. I don't let him too close because, if I do, Jane feels she will be crushed and dominated. I keep men away by keeping Jane busy and overweight."

Next, create two columns on a blank page. At the top of the first column write "What my defense protects me from"; at the top of the second, "What my defense does not allow me to have." Fill in each column as it relates to the information that came out of the "shield" entry.

BONDING WITH THE SOUL

SHAME

Reflection: First, accept that shame is different from guilt. Guilt is an attitude about something, and shame is an attitude about self.

- Allow yourself to locate and see clearly the attitude of shame that you carry.

- Notice what methods you use to push down or try to get rid of the feeling.

- Observe how you cope mentally with the feeling of shame.

- What do you do with the feeling when it arises?

Journal: Draw an abstract image of your inner stockpile or reservoir of shame. Inside it write a word or phrase about a few pockets of shame that you hide. Outside your drawing make little circles. Next to each circle write a word or phrase that other people say that has the power to push your shame buttons. Now, connect the button-pushing phrases with the hidden shame on the inside of your drawing. Notice how a seemingly innocent phrase can so quickly draw you into such a painful place. You may choose to share what the diagram has revealed with a trusted person.

8
Passages

BIRTH

*Ho! All ye of the heavens, all ye of the air, all ye of the
earth,
I bid you all to hear me!
Into your midst has come a new life.
Consent ye, consent ye all, I implore! make its path
smooth—
then it shall travel beyond the four hills!*

Prayer from Omaha Indian ceremony for the newborn

The birth of our first child put everything else in our world into
a different perspective. Suddenly there was a little baby girl in our
midst who gave meaning to everything just by being there. The
motions of her little arms and legs, the look in her eyes and her various cries had more power to mobilize us on every level than anything that had ever happened before. Suddenly we were parents. It
was time to put our lives in order, be a family, create a home,
become grown-ups, follow a routine, change wardrobes. In short, it
was time to do anything and everything necessary to rise to this awe-
some challenge.

Our daughter won "The Prettiest Baby in the Nursery" prize, an
honor bestowed by the nurses, three days in a row. She was an
angel. She had huge eyes, rosebud lips, and she held her little fist to
her chin as if she was in deep thought. After
about three days this little angel, who had not
made a peep, began to cry. I sat up in my
hospital bed dumbfounded, frozen in terror. I
couldn't think of a thing to do. My husband
stood and stared, looking as horrified as I felt. Suddenly he broke his
pose, walked over to the bed and picked her up. He played with her
and bounced her on his shoulder and she was content again. I

*Man always dies
before he is fully
born.*

Erich Fromm

thought he was a genius. I couldn't imagine how he had thought of that. What a brilliant guy I had married!

If ever we think we have ourselves together, the birth of our first child alters that self-concept radically. If we have a shred of arrogance, a baby will set us straight. We will know anxiety we hadn't dreamed possible. We will bite our nails, wring our hands and knock on wood. We will understand feeling vulnerable because suddenly what was inside and protected is now a separate life, and that life that is more important than our own is now subject to the elements. All of our biological systems are on red-alert 24 hours a day to protect this little life, keep it safe and hold it in the soul of the Divine.

> *The child is an inner possibility, the possibility of renewal.*
>
> Marie Louise von Franz

To bond at this level we must open secret doors within the self that may never have swung free before, reaching beyond what we thought we were to know ourselves in a different way. It asks us to clean house; to free the self of the contaminants that will inhibit this process; to search our souls for unfinished business and finish it so we won't impose it on this new life; to face our deepest demons; and to make room for more joy than we have ever known.

This is birth. It happens when we have children. It also happens within the self, with ideas, life decisions and the birth of the soul nature. Birth is a process that continues throughout life, an awakening to a new dimension of aliveness, a welcoming and nurturing of new life, life in any and all of its forms. It reminds us what a sacred path we are on when we choose to be alive or to give life to another.

❧

No single event can awaken within us a stranger totally unknown to us. To live is to be slowly born.

Antoine de Saint-Exupéry

ADOLESCENCE

Do not mistake a child for his symptom.

Erik Erikson

I was in my room one evening when the phone rang for my teenage daughter.

"Is Marina there?" asked her friend.

"Yes," I replied, "did you try her line?"

"I did," explained the friend, "but she left a message on her machine saying that she had left her room."

Marina's room is her home within our home, and her level of contact with her friends is such that she would not want to be unavailable for the time that it takes to bake a cake. I thought of the family answering machine that has had the same message on it for eight years. I remembered that it took us the better part of an evening to figure it all out. Technology has certainly changed, but perhaps the developmental tasks of a teenager are still much as I remember.

Adolescence and teenage years provide for the dawning, organizing and practicing of a self separate from the parents, a self that is not dependent on the parent for survival.

Around 12 years of age children begin to move from concrete to abstract thinking. They can entertain ideas and concepts that are not attached to actual objects. They can conceptualize a separate self that is autonomous, different from the parent. Much energy in teenage years goes toward securing a place for that self in the outside world. The peer group becomes all-important, providing a surrogate family to create a safe passage from the family to society at large. This is a stage of individuation.

Individuation leads to self-actualization and soul growth. People who are well-individuated and have intact identities and coherent selves are best equipped to take charge of their own lives, to form meaningful long-term relationships and to choose a life's work or path. They will be in a position to know themselves, to observe their own thoughts and make constructive inner correlations and conclusions that will be helpful to them. If they have a solid sense of self, they will be able to understand better the social dynamics around them. They will know that they are connected but separate; that they are individuals and will be able to position themselves better and in more positive ways in relation to other people. Without a sense of an individual self, their self-thoughts will always feel dependent upon what others think.

That is why it is so important that parents of teenagers give them the message that they can *separate and still stay connected.* If children are punished for attempting to separate from their parents and given covert messages that if they separate, they will lose their parents' love and support, they won't know that it's okay to be different from their parents. As parents, we get so attached to caring for our children that we don't want to let go of that control, but really it is only the illusion of control.

Our children are in charge of themselves, and it is our job to support them in their autonomy, to love them, not as extensions of ourselves but as separate people. They have been profoundly connected to us and they remain profoundly connected, but now as individuals, as people who connect with self and soul from their own position in this world, who are beings within and unto themselves.

❧

He who would learn to fly one day must first learn to stand and walk and run and climb and dance: one cannot fly into flying.

Friedrich Nietzsche

MID-LIFE

And we may start to feel that this is a time of always letting go, of one thing after another after another, our waistlines, our vigor, our sense of adventure, our 20/20 vision, our trust in justice, our earnestness, our playfulness, our dream of being a tennis star, or a TV star, or a senator. . . . We feel shaken. We feel scared. We do not feel safe. The center's not holding and things are falling apart. All of a sudden our friends, if not us, are having affairs, divorces, heart attacks, cancer. Some of our friends—men and women our age!—have died. And as we acquire new aches and new pains, our health care is, of necessity, being supplied by internists, cardiologists, dermatologists, podiatrists, urologists, periodontists, gynecologists and psychiatrists, from all of whom we want a second opinion.
We want a second opinion that says, don't worry, you are going to live forever.

Judith Viorst, *Necessary Losses*

When I was 35 years old, I was diagnosed with cancer. I thought the doctor must be talking about someone else. I felt too young. I was just getting going in life. I had two beautiful children and a young, successful husband. This wasn't supposed to happen. When I told my mother, she said, "Boy! Life's what happens to you when you're making other plans." It felt right.

The night before my operation, my doctor rattled off a lot of statistics. I went from just fine to dead in 60 seconds. When I asked him where on the continuum I might fall, he said, "Listen, we're all terminal in this room; you just found out about it a little sooner than the rest of us." His words floated down to the bottom of my soul. They were both a sentence and a reprieve, terror and relief, bondage and liberation.

Those words began a subtle shift that affected all my life, a shift in the relative importance of things. I stopped doing what didn't feel life-enhancing and did more of what felt meaningful. Slowly I let go of living to please or impress a silent majority that I would never meet. I came to understand that what I didn't do now, while it presented itself to me, I may not have another opportunity to do. I still get tears in my eyes when I read Emily's words from the last act of Thornton Wilder's *Our Town*:

> *"We don't have time to look at one another. . . . I didn't realize it. So all that was going on and we never noticed. . . . Oh, earth, you're too wonderful for anybody to realize you. . . . Do any human beings ever realize life while they live it?"*

Now I feel lucky. Cancer let me know that I was going to die, but then I went on living; that is a privilege, to be alive and healthy and to know every day that life is not permanent. It changes everything. It took away my innocence but it gave me wisdom. I value life differently now because I know that one day I will lose it, and I value relationships because I know that they are temporary.

Mid-life transition begins with the dawning of the awareness that life will not last forever. Generally, our awareness is at least partly unconscious. If it were fully conscious, we would go into therapy and embark on a true search for self, soul and meaning. When it is less than conscious, we do a variety of dramatic things to reassure ourselves that we are still young, that we are masters of our fate, invincible, that we look tired, not old. In short, that we will forever. This is the season of affairs, sports cars, hairpieces, aerobics, divorces and other manifestations of the last gasp of youth, the wish for a second chance.

Mid-life crisis can also be precipitated by achieving ambitions and discovering that they are wanting, by getting there and finding that there's not there. This is when a true relationship with soul can begin because one learns, first-hand, that the things and experiences of the world do not actually hold what they seemed to promise, that a life of enhanced self- and soul-awareness, as well as waking up to the beauty and meaning of relationships, is what it's all about. Mid-life crisis is an important opportunity to put one's self and life into good and satisfying order in preparation for a happy and fulfilling second half of life. It is precipitated by deep and real issues and longings. If faced and worked with, they enable us to move into the next stages of life, greater understanding of self, and a deeper sense of appreciation of what life can and cannot offer.

The task of mid-life is to finish old business so it does not keep us from getting what we need as we move on. Many people at this stage gain a new awareness of people and society and begin to branch out in altruistic ways. Many life tasks have been accomplished and energies are freed up for introspection. It is a time when not only the question of, but the need for soul arises. It is an inner thirst, a self wishing to be revealed, a heart wanting to know itself and in knowing itself, recognizing the other.

❦

A child-like man is not a man whose development has been arrested; on the contrary, he is a man who has given himself a chance of continuing to develop long after most adults have muffled themselves in the cocoon of middle-aged habit and convention.

Aldous Huxley

MATURITY

Nothing is inherently and invincibly young except spirit. And spirit can enter a human being perhaps better in the quiet of old age and dwell there more undisturbed than in the turmoil of adventure.

George Santayana

Accumulating years in the act of living is no guarantee of maturity. In fact, it is possible to be born, grow old and die without ever maturing.

Maturity includes being able to dwell in the center of the self, with a balanced perspective. It is taking time to be alone and time to be with others. It is knowing what is really important in life, and not losing sight of that because of some piece of glitter that offers itself as a panacea or an intoxication. Maturity is knowing our real place in the world and feeling comfortable with it.

Becoming mature does not mean we will no longer feel needy or wish, occasionally, to fall apart. Maturity does not guarantee that we will not have bouts of insecurity or go through periods of deep confusion. Nor does it mean that we are no longer examining the self or exploring the life of the soul. Real maturity calls on us to exercise a kind of self-acceptance that allows both strengths and weaknesses, neither crucifying ourselves for our flaws nor becoming grandiose about our strengths.

Before enlightenment, carry the water, till the soil.
After enlightenment, carry the water, till the soil.

Zen proverb

Maturity is what allows us to live the life we have and not postpone that living for the dream or fantasy of another life. It allows us enough inner quiet to experience soul—to devote the time it takes, to give up the bondage and attachments to unlived lives and let go of the regrets of what never was and may never be. Maturity allows us to live in the moment because it recognizes that the moment is all we have within our reach, and that it is, after all is said and done, enough.

Whatever is formed for long duration arrives slowly to its maturity.

Samuel Johnson

❧

Maturity consists in no longer being taken in by oneself.

Kajetan von Schlaggenberg

DEATH

He may cry for rest, peace, and dignity, but he will get infusions, transfusions, a heart machine, or a tracheotomy if necessary. . . . Is this approach our own way to cope with and repress the anxieties that a terminally ill or critically ill patient evokes in us? Is our concentration on equipment, on blood pressure, our desperate attempt to deny the impending death which is so frightening and discomforting to us that we displace all our knowledge onto machines, since they are less close to us than the suffering face of another human being which would remind us once more of our lack of omnipotence, our own limits and failures, and last but not least our own mortality?

from *On Death and Dying*, by Elizabeth Kübler-Ross

When we come to terms with our own inevitable death, we come to terms with life. Until we glimpse immortality, which is also the realm of spirit, soul is only a word.

Most of us live as if death were never going to come. We take life for granted, even at times wishing it away. We avoid talking or thinking about death, and when we are forced to deal with it, we treat it as something unpleasant, even a rudeness, as though someone belched at the dinner table. Until someone close to us dies. Then we realize that we are not all-powerful. Then we get in touch with our own powerlessness over the inevitable and we get a glimpse of true surrender.

We surrender our idea that somehow we will be the ones who will beat the odds, who will live forever. We surrender our fantasy that we will lead such an exciting, enriching life that we will eradicate anything undesirable from it. We surrender our need for supreme control because we recognize that over the most important question, our own death, we have no control at all. When we surrender the illusion that we can control others, we also come to understand that we are mortals among mortals and no matter how

Only those are fit to live who do not fear to die; and none are fit to die who have shrunk from the joy of life and the duty of life. Both life and death are parts of the same Great Adventure.

Theodore Roosevelt

deeply we love, no matter how important others are to us, their lives and deaths, as well as our own, are out of our hands.

Though this knowledge of our own mortality is in some sense an awful and a painful recognition, it is also a spiritual liberation. If we know that we do not have forever to live, why waste precious time trying to beat the clock? Why be with people we don't connect with or care about, do work that feels hollow *In the midst of life we are in death.*

The Book of Common Prayer

and meaningless, or look into the faces of those to whom we are supposedly the closest and realize that we hardly see them? Why live life as if we had time to waste, love to squander and relationships to throw away?

Accepting our own mortality also allows us to recognize that all we really have is today, that the here and now is all that exists for sure. When we come fully into touch with this truth, our experience of life transforms around us. We see things with new eyes and a new sense of appreciation. The very colors that we look at seem to have a subtle luminescence that was not there when we did not bring our full being and attendance to the present moment. When we know that the relationships in our lives will not last forever, we come to a direct appreciation for their real meaning to us and become less demanding and exacting. When we come into touch with our own inevitable death, we feel that we have been given a second chance at life because now we hold each moment of it in our hands as something precious, something to be placed in the center of our palm while we look admiringly at it.

Death and life, life and death. We cannot truly see one until we have seen the other.

❦

Death has to be waiting at the end of the ride,
before you truly see the earth, and feel your heart, and love the world.

Jean Anouilh

MOURNING

All changes, even the most longed for, have their melancholy, for what we leave behind us is a part of ourselves; we must die to one life before we can enter into another.

Anatole France

I was eating red Jell-O with Cool Whip in the hospital cafeteria when the announcement came over the loudspeaker to go to the ICU. My father had waited for me to leave and then he quietly slipped away. It was over. He wasn't in pain anymore. I knew as I walked up the stairs that when I got into the room my father would no longer be there. His body lay very still but his soul had flown away. How strange his body looked without him in it, so empty, so left behind, just a fleshy container that used to house him, he who was half of the whole universe, who filled an entire state just with his presence. I wanted to fly up, too, to find him in the sky and take his hand for one more walk, to touch his cheek, to smell him. I needed to hear his voice, but it would never come from his body again.

My father was dead. Somehow I would have to find a way to live in this world without him. The impossible had happened; an era was ending. I felt a chapter in my life close forever. I would never be able to read those pages with him again. Goodbye, Papa. I will miss you.

There is no avoiding loss in life. Life is a taking on and a letting go of experience, and each experience we let go of has a component of loss. Remember when you were a child on a vacation? You accepted your vacation world as a new universe to explore, making new friends, learning new things, getting attached to a new environment. When it came time to leave, you thought you could never live without it. As we grow older we understand the temporary nature of a vacation, and so we recognize even while we are enjoying it that it will not last forever.

Mourning, the psyche's natural healing aid in coping with any sort of loss, is a crucial part of the letting-go process. We think of mourning as being connected only to death, but it is connected to losses of all kinds. When we do not allow ourselves to mourn, the painful feelings fester. If we do not mourn the loss of our own youth, we may resent those who are young. If we have a friend who moves out of town and do not mourn the loss of that friendship, every time we have the chance to make new friends we will be afraid to get close for fear of losing them. If we do not mourn the loss of family in divorce, we will not dare commit our hearts again.

Our society, unfortunately, does not allow much room for mourning. Paradoxically, as our need for mourning and grieving increases through longer life expectancy and more mobile lifestyles, our vehicles for mourning seem to be decreasing. The most obvious of these is the funeral. Where once the funeral was a ritual that allowed active mourning, today it discourages overt grief. If a person who has suffered a loss still seems sad a few months later, we want him or her to move on and get back to life; we are impatient with continued sadness.

Until relatively recently, most religions set aside the year following a death as the period of mourning. During that period the grieving individuals would wear black to let the world know that they were carrying a special wound and needed a particular kind of patience and care. At the end of the year, a ceremony would signal their return to life. Throughout the year, people were expected to understand that these individuals had undergone a major loss and needed time to adjust and heal.

When we do not mourn a deep loss fully, we condemn the unconscious to hold the magnitude of that pain and loss somewhere within itself. For the rest of our lives, each time we encounter an experience of intimacy that because of its depth of caring threatens to expose the wound to our conscious mind, we have to walk away. We walk away from ourselves, from the relationship, from our potential for love and life. We cannot go to that place of pain again, not because it hurt so much, but because we did not let it hurt enough. If we do not grieve, losing someone we love—whether through death, divorce or disease—becomes a loss of ourselves.

The mourning process is in itself a giving in to tragedy—to the depth of the loss, to the full extent of the pain. Only when we pass through what feels like a sort of personal death can we return fully to life. If we will experience only part of the loss, then part of ourselves remains locked in the frozen silence of unfelt sadness which will leave us shut down; we will be less alive within ourselves and our daily living. We will have that much less of ourselves available to us in our daily lives.

The need to grieve is as old as humanity. Grief, fully and purely experienced, allows us to go on with life, to pass through all the stages of anger, sadness, justifying and letting go. It creates space for new life to be born out of the wreckage of the past, and for a new person to be born out of the previous one. In mourning we reach the parameters of our soul—we die an emotional death and are resuscitated. Deep, pure grieving allows us to integrate the loss because nothing we have truly loved is ever really completely lost to us. When we refuse to grieve it, we put the loss out of consciousness; numb, we cannot gain access to either the good or the bad feelings surrounding the loss or person. When we feel all our feelings, we are able to choose what to keep alive in memory, what to continue to look at and feel nourished by.

❦

Drink and sing,
an inch before us is black night.

Japanese proverb

HOW DO WE GRIEVE?

Since every death diminishes us a little,
we grieve—not so much for the death
as for ourselves.

Lynn Caine, *Widow*

Where does the grief, sadness, anger and fear go when we as a society no longer honor the depth of a loss and support each other through it? We seem to regard feelings of grief as a sign of weakness rather than strength. In fact, true grieving requires a strong ego and

This only is denied to God: the power to undo the past.

Agathon

helps to build a strong ego because it asks us to stand within our pain and yield to it. It asks us to be strong and compassionate and wise enough to hold our own woundedness in our hearts without abandoning ourselves

at this very crucial moment. There is nothing weak about that; it is a sign of love and contact with what is real and alive in this world, and it requires wisdom to give ourselves the right to be real.

John Bowlby feels that separation is "biologically programmed," and he outlines four stages of mourning: (1) numbing; (2) yearning, searching and anger; (3) disorganization and despair; and (4) reorganization. The first stage may be an apparent calmness and is based on emotional shutdown in which all feelings are suppressed, all reality denied, until the bereaved person is in a safe enough situation to let go a little.

In the second stage the person searches back through past events to something that could have been done differently. Anger is also a natural part of this stage, and the expression of the anger—whether it is at a person, a system, a society—is part of what will help the person to accept the loss eventually.

In the third and fourth stages, the mourner faces the fact that the very person relied on for hope and comfort in the face of a major loss is now unavailable. Eventually, however, through true mourning, the bereaved person begins once more to build up his or her inner world.

At the turn of this century, the average life expectancy was 36 years. Today, the average person has a life expectancy of 76 years. Learning to let go of one stage in life and move into another is not a luxury but a necessity for ongoing health and happiness.

Passing wholly through the stages of grief, loss and mourning— whether it be for a loved one, a beloved object, a job, a child who has left home, a stage of life—not only strength-ens the ego and the inner self, but increases our trust in life's ability to repair and renew itself. It deepens our inner relationship with the self and the experiences and objects that we carry within our own psyche, which further paves the path toward spirit and deepens the soul connection.

> *Do as the heavens have done, forget your evil; With them forgive yourself.*
>
> William Shakespeare

Grief serves a number of important functions. It releases the pain surrounding an event or situation so that it will not be held within the psyche, the emotional and physical self. Grief allows the wound to heal. If we do not grieve, we build walls around the ungrieved wound in order to protect it. When a wound is not healed, it hurts. It is tender to the touch; so we push away any experience that might touch it, press on it or produce pain.

Experiencing the deep pain of grief makes it easier not to retreat from deep experience when it presents itself again in our lives. We reduce the fear that we will not be able to handle the potential pain that could be associated with deep feeling and caring. Grief is nec-essary in order to release the anger—at feeling helpless and out of control, or at losing something or someone important—that arises as part of the grieving process so that we can risk loving or becoming attached again in life.

If we cannot mourn, a number of things happen to us. We stay stuck in anger and pain. We cannot engage in new relationships because we are still engaged in an active relationship with a person that is no longer present. We project unfelt, unresolved grief onto any situation, placing those feelings where they do not belong. We lose personal history along with the unmourned person or situation—a part of us dies, too. And we unconsciously fear losing our next similar relationship—hence any important relationship can become fearsome.

A surprisingly large number of life events go ungrieved in our futile attempt to "get on with life" or to "stop feeling sorry for ourselves." These include: divorce, both for spouses, children and the family unit; life transitions; loss of job, youth, children in the home; retirement; dysfunction in the home, loss of family life; lost childhood, lost security, constant abandonment, loss of parents who were able to behave like parents.

Mourning has at the end of it great optimism. By allowing this process to run its full course we can continue to engage and reengage in life as it presents itself to us in a variety of forms, over and over again. Mourning can teach us the great lesson that everything is temporary. When we understand this and keep it in the front of our minds, not only does our experience of life transform, so does our ability to enjoy it: we come to see and understand life's true value. When we truly mourn, truly experience the love and the loss, then we mourn not just with our minds and emotions, but with our soul.

❦

Let mourning stop when one's grief is fully expressed.

Confucius

BONDING WITH THE SOUL

MOURNING A PERSON

Reflection: Think of someone about whom you feel unusual pain, or perhaps a loss that is left unmourned or unreconciled because the circumstances surrounding the loss didn't allow it, or because you couldn't endure the painful feelings. The loss can be through death, separation or even as a result of disease. Answer these questions, either through personal dialogue or in your journal:

 What is the person's name?

 What was he or she like before the loss?

 Recall an incident or aspect of the relationship that has special meaning for you.

 What part of yourself do you need to retrieve that you lost when you lost the person?

 Do you carry feelings of loss for what might have been and never got a chance to be?

 If so, do you feel those feelings now?

Journal: In your journal say goodbye to this person in whatever way feels appropriate. Do you want to thank this person for being in your life? (In cases where the separation is hostile it can be healing to reconnect with what was good and beautiful as well as what didn't work.) If so, include that in your journal entry.

BONDING WITH THE SOUL

Loss of a Person

Reflections: We can lose a person in many ways, to death, divorce, separation, addiction or physical disease. In your mind, allow the person you lost to come into focus. Answer these questions:

- How did you lose this person?

- When did it happen or begin to happen?

- What was happening in your life around this time?

- How old were you?

- Where did you live?

- What were you not able to say then that you would like to say now?

- What are the treasures that you keep with you from this relationship?

- What do you keep that you would like to release?

Journal: Write an epitaph for this person, or write him or her a letter saying all the things that you wish you had said but weren't able to. Sign it, then read it back to yourself or to someone you trust. Do not send it. This letter is only for your personal work.

BONDING WITH THE SOUL

DEATH

Reflection: Allow yourself to be with a person whom you have lost to death, divorce, disease or separation. Let her or him come fully to mind; see, feel and talk in your imagination with this person.

Journal: When you feel ready, write a letter to this person. Say all that you need to say to express your feelings. Tell or describe how you experienced him or her: your joy, your sorrow, your anger, your hurt, your companionship. Tell her or him what you miss most and what you don't miss. Be specific. You may say goodbye if you wish in any way that helps you to come to closure, remembering that you will always carry this person within you. Tell the person what parts of him or her you wish to keep and what you might like to let go of.

You may reverse roles with this person and write a letter you would like to receive in response to your letter. Don't mail either letter. This is for your use only.

BONDING WITH SOUL

CHILDHOOD/ADOLESCENCE/TEENAGE YEARS

Reflection: Allow yourself to scroll back through time to a period in life that speaks to you or draws you in some way.

- How did your life feel?

- What were your pleasures?

- What were your fears?

- What were your dreams?

- When you looked at your family, what did you see?

- How did you feel about your position in the family? How did you experience it?

Journal: If you are a parent of a child, adolescent, teenager or mature child, write two journal entries. First, write to yourself at the age your child is now, i.e., the adult you writes an entry to the adolescent you. Then reverse roles, and write as yourself at that age.

Second, reverse roles with your child today and write an entry as if you are your child. Try to get into his or her head and speak *as* him or her.

Now, read over the entries. Are any of your unresolved feelings about yourself, when you were the age corresponding to your child's age, mixed with or projected onto your child today? How are the entries similar? How are they different? Remembering that your child is not you, were you able to reverse roles with him or her?

BONDING WITH THE SOUL

ADOLESCENCE

Reflection: Looking through a scrapbook or collection of pictures, find a photograph of yourself during adolescence that speaks to you in some way. Or perhaps you have clearly in mind an image of yourself as an adolescent. Look at the picture or image and answer these questions:

ᴥ What were your concerns?

ᴥ What were your worries?

ᴥ What did you experience the most fun doing?

ᴥ What else gave you pleasure?

ᴥ What about yourself made you feel good?

ᴥ What about yourself embarrassed you?

ᴥ When you looked at your family and your position in your family at that time, what did you see?

ᴥ What was your school experience?

Journal: With adolescence comes the dawning of abstract thinking and the ability to move from concrete to abstract thought. At this point we begin to have the ability to reflect or separate ourselves from our surroundings. This can feel both lonely and liberating. As you began to separate from your family and look back at it as a separate person, what did you see? Write a journal entry describing your observations.

BONDING WITH THE SOUL

MID-LIFE

Reflection: Mid-life crisis is a moment when we can look back and see how far we have come, and then look forward to see where we need to go. With mortality in sight, we are motivated to finish old business that we no longer want to drag along, and we wish to move into our dreams. We are aware that if we don't do it now, we probably won't do it at all.

- What are three experiences you would like to have?

- What areas of your life or relationship do you need to finish?

- What might stand in the way of that accomplishment?

Journal: What is something that you would like to do that you have never done? Learn to play tennis? Write a children's book? Volunteer at a charity kitchen? Change professions? Whatever it is, write it in your journal.

Next, write out three to five steps that you need to take to get closer to making your dream a reality.

9
Balance

BALANCING THE INNER AND THE OUTER WORLD

When you make the two one, and when you make the inner as the outer and the outer as the inner and the above as the below . . . then shall you enter the Kingdom.

The Gospel According to Thomas

Balance is an inner experience that allows thought, feeling and action to be integrated. Living at the extremes is tempting, whether at the ascetic end or the daredevil extreme, but living at the still centerpoint puts us in contact with our soul.

When Buddha was a young ascetic he did endless practices in order to find God. He denied himself food, comfort and shelter in an attempt to rely only on the divine and, in a sense, humiliate the flesh, until one day he heard a musician offering a teaching to his student. The musician was showing the student how to string his instrument and he said, "If you string too tight it will break. If you leave it too loose, you cannot play it." Immediately, the young Buddha realized that he was developing a human instrument that could not play music. He was living in such an extreme way that he had lost access to himself.

Bringing our inner and outer worlds into balance is an important step in the abundant expression of soul. As children, most of us were not afraid to let our inner selves show. But as awareness of the outside world increased, we learned to edit our interior to fit into our perception of what was expected and accepted on the outside. Though this is a natural process, it can cause us to lose touch with our inner selves.

At the still point of the turning world . . .
Neither from nor towards; at the still point, there the dance is. . . .

T. S. Eliot, "Burnt Norton"

An easy and natural flow from the inner to the outer world is necessary for soul's expression because soul flows from within and is fed from both within and without. Children often use transitional objects—teddy bears, pacifiers, blankets, even their parents—to keep their connection with their inner worlds alive as they extend themselves into the outside world. Adults may use mood-altering substances such as liquor to connect their inner and outer worlds comfortably, but these artificial means do not allow them to achieve a true balance.

While we live comparing our interior selves with other people's exteriors, we become increasingly disconnected with our inner nature and dependent on the assessment and opinions of others to tell us who we are.

When we learn how to be comfortable with what is inside of us and to allow more of that person to shine through into day-to-day living, we become more truly independent and in a stronger position to allow soul to be part of our lives.

🌿

That which oppresses me, is it my soul
trying to come out in the open,
or the soul of the world knocking
at my heart for its entrance.

Rabindranath Tagore

BALANCING THE MASCULINE AND THE FEMININE

When opposites no longer damage each other,
Both are benefited through the attainment of Tao. . . .
Therefore the wise identifies opposites as one,
And sets an example for the world.

Tao Te Ching

In most times and places in history, clear gender-role delineation was appropriate. But this is increasingly not the case in our contemporary world. Today we are finding that women can run corporations and men can nurture children, and the world continues to spin on its axis. Many people in modern society are finding to their delight that when they bring their roles into balance, they also bring themselves into balance.

The freedom and ability to experience and express both our masculine and our feminine sides allow us to be both creative and strong, vulnerable and controlled, nurturing and aggressive. We do not have to give up one for the other. Making room for the masculine and the feminine to coexist within each person, man or woman, creates greater freedom of expression and more life choices, and ultimately allows us to be at peace with ourselves. Men can be men and still have a gentle or intuitive side, and women can be women but still enjoy their aggressive, competent and outwardly powerful aspect. Men can cook and women can play ball.

This rebalancing is life-changing and world-changing. We find that we can look within for nurturing and motivation. Balancing the masculine and feminine also helps to heal society by restoring the equilibrium of values, feminizing the workplace and government, and bringing paternal influence back to the intimate arena of the home.

❧

He who knows the masculine and yet keeps to the feminine
will become a channel drawing all the world towards it.

Ch'u Ta-kao

JOY

Man is fond of counting his troubles, but he does not count his joys. If he counted them up as he ought to, he would see that every lot has enough happiness provided for it.

Fyodor Dostoyevski

The sun
Breaks out
And sears
The drifts
Of cloud
That float
Along

The shroud
No longer
Low-lies.

The note
Of the song
Of the bird
Is heard.

The cloud
Is furled.

Earth cries
A shout
Of gladness

O'er skies,
And trees,
And leaf,
And leaves
Of bay
Breaks day

e.e. cummings

The experience of joy implies an acceptance of our inner life and the surrounding world. Joy asks us to be willing to accept life on its own terms. A sense of joy in life allows a certain freedom of movement, a detachment from the daily aggravations or those minor disappointments that arise from being overly attached to a thousand little objects and events.

Joy is a state of awareness, a continually renewing state of mind. It carries with it a sense of good fortune and blessing. Joy is a self-generating experience. It can be brought into being through a disciplined awareness of its presence, through allowing and invoking it into consciousness.

Joy is self-directed. It allows life to be what it is. Often it is the result of an inner decision to bring it into being. If we have choices in life, then why not choose joy? Joy understands that life is not necessarily here to please us. It is not beholden. Its job is not to fulfill all our wishes and desires.

Joy asks us to recognize that the events of life are not the source of joy, that instead joy rises out of the experience of self or soul rather than an external object. To be joyful is to invite soul to manifest. It allows the experiencer to see beauty in what is rather than what she wishes to see. Joy is a lightness of being that enables us to sense and appreciate the subtle beauty that surrounds us and to hear the quiet voice of soul in all that exists.

❦

All joys want eternity,
Want deep, profound eternity.

Friedrich Nietzsche

LOVE

It is what we all do with our hearts that affects others most deeply. It is not the movements of our body or the words within our mind that transmit love. We love from heart to heart.

Gerald G. Jampolsky, M.D.

Just as the Eskimos have many words for snow, the ancient Greeks had many words for love. Perhaps during the Golden Age of Greece, people experienced more love and so were able to linger longer with its various manifestations and gradations. Just as the Eskimos need to identify many forms of snow, perhaps the Greeks needed to distinguish and name many forms of what they observed within and around them.

Based on this theme, John Lee in *The Colors of Love* distinguishes between six types of love.

Eros is a romantic and sexual love, a need to know everything about the loved one and to experience her or him fully. *Mania* is an obsessive and demanding love, often accompanied by pain and anxiety because the

There is a land of the living and a land of the dead and the bridge is love, the only survival, the only meaning.

Thornton Wilder, The Bridge of San Luis Rey

need for attention from the other is insatiable. *Ludis* is a self-centered, playful love; love is treated as a game to be won. *Storge* is a companionate love, a solid peaceful love between close friends. *Agape* is a saintly "thou" centered love, always patient, forgiving and kind. *Pragma* is practical and logical love, given only after one has determined whether or not the partner is a "good catch."

In our society we seem to value *eros*, or romantic love, most. When this happens, it negatively impacts long-term relationships because when we lose or move past the romantic stage of love, we often feel we have lost *the* love in the relationship. While it is good to keep romantic love alive in a relationship, a relationship—in order to last—will also need to include other forms of love, such as *storge* (or filial love) and *agape*. These other forms of love will supply the relationship with the friendship and the spirituality it needs to live, grow and sustain itself through life. They will also incorporate romance in a manner that feeds rather than drains intimacy.

Love has power that dispels Death;
Charm that conquers the enemy.
Kahlil Gibran

Love, particularly *agape*, aligns us with soul energy because more than a sentiment, it is a state of awareness. To enter into a state of love is to be present with soul. Soul and life and love are somehow together; enter one and you are with the others.

Love also has a physical side. The heart has 40 to 60 times the electrical impulse of the brain. What the heart experiences is communicated to every cell in your body. If you are upset, for example, your whole body feels it.

According to Donna Willis, M.D., experiencing the feeling of love has a biochemical effect. When we do not experience love in our lives, our immune system is decreased which undermines our first line of defense against illness. When we can relax and calm the heart, it can capture our two nervous systems and make them operate in a smooth and efficient manner, which in turn lowers our blood pressure. If you can calm down you heart, it sends a message to the brain and calms it. The brain then sends a message of calm throughout the body.

Dr. Willis suggests that when we are upset, we follow these simple steps in order to restore ourselves to a calm state: (1) Recognize what is distressing us, i.e., losing our keys, a sick child, a problem at home or at work, etc.; (2) Pause; (3) Shift our focus from our mind to our heart, center ourselves through breathing and breathe from the heart for about ten seconds; (4) Recall a time when we felt loved and appreciated and image it in our mind.

To move toward love is to invite an energy state into being, to manifest soul. All that is necessary to alter our state of awareness is calm, relaxation and a mental attitude that serenely expects love's energy to be present. Love becomes the center from which we experience both our self and our surroundings. Our life may not change fundamentally, but our experience of it will alter.

This is what the ordinary soul is all about—seeing through the lens of soul, being anchored from within the heart rather than chasing the shadows of the mind, spending time within the equanimity of the soul rather than wasting endless hours preoccupied and anxious. Love is available to us at all times. It is that soul space within each of us where all the waters meet.

*It is only with the heart that one can see rightly what is essential
is invisible to the eye.*

Antoine de Saint-Exupéry

BONDING WITH THE SOUL

FEELING LOVE

Reflection: Think of times when you feel loved and appreciated. Allow yourself to have full body recall of those feelings and observe how feeling loved and feeling love affect your body, your breathing and your overall sense of well-being. How does this feeling of love affect your thinking? How does it affect the way that you see yourself and the situation you are in?

Journal: In your journal begin with the sentence, "When I am loved I feel . . ." Take your time to create within you the feeling of being loved and appreciated. Once you are in this state of mind, complete the sentence by recording the physical and emotional feelings you are having when you rest in the physical and emotional experiences of love. You may also wish to note down how resting in the experience of love affects your thinking and perception of your day or of a particular situation. Note that you put yourself into this physical and emotional state of feeling love by creating it in your mind.

BONDING WITH THE SOUL

TRANSFORMATION

Reflection: Make yourself comfortable and relaxed and take a moment to reflect on the following questions. What were the turnoffs you experienced as a child related to spirituality? What were disillusioning spiritual experiences you had, if any, that made you lose faith? What were some inspiring spiritual experiences that led you to have faith?

Journal: In the center of a piece of paper, draw a circle that represents your personal core sense of spirituality. Inside and around the circle, use phrases or words that describe situations or times in which you feel connected with soul and spirituality.

Now, just outside of that, write the names of activities that put you in touch with your spiritual self or soul nature, such as meditation, nature walks, religious observances, or whatever feels like it engenders a feeling of spirituality and a closeness with soul.

Outside of those activities, write what interferes with these soulful activities. It may be busyness, a feeling they lead nowhere, a feeling of being undeserving or a lack of time. Whatever it is for you, write it down so you can see it in front of you.

Now, go back to your diagram and choose two or three activities that you would like to do more often in your daily life. Write them down.

Make a contract with yourself as to how you will bring those activities into your life more regularly.

BONDING WITH THE SOUL

BALANCE

Reflection: Close your eyes and let yourself imagine yourself first as a child, then an adolescent, then a teenager, then an adult. Throughout these stages you will have both masculine and feminine sides to your character. Just observe these various qualities as they arise in your consciousness.

Journal: In your journal make two columns. At the top of one column write the word "masculine," and at the top of the other column write the word "feminine." In the appropriate columns, list the qualities that you feel to be aspects of masculinity and of femininity. Place a check mark next to the qualities in either column that you feel you have. Then ask yourself:

- How do I feel about the qualities I have from the opposite-gender column?

- Which ones bother me, and why?

- What are my opposite-gender strengths?

- Do I have the right to these opposite-gender qualities?

- How can I integrate and express those qualities to bring me into greater balance and contentment?

10
Play

THE IMPORTANCE OF PLAY

If a man insisted always on being serious, and never allowed himself a bit of fun and relaxation, he would go mad or become unstable without knowing it.

Herodotus

When our son was six or so, he had a friend who lived on the top of a small mountain with whom he adored playing. There were newborn kittens snuggled into a hollow tree, streams to skip stones in and woods to explore. They saw themselves as Huck Finn and Tom Sawyer. They felt the call of the wild and the mystery of the forest. We would drop our son off at nine or ten in the morning and let him stay until dusk; but when we picked him up he would look at us with dismay and say, "I just got here, I'm not ready to go yet." His engagement in the experience of play released him into a world where time did not exist.

Today, we think of play as something children do. But this has not always been the case. For centuries, there was little distinction made between children and adults. They performed the same work, sang the same songs and played the same games. With the rise of the merchant class in the 17th century and afterward, however, the work ethic became central to the "serious adult," and play was eventually relegated to childhood. In that relegation we lost an ancient pathway to soul.

Play has profound implications on the path toward soulful living. It dislodges the rigid and fixed attitudes that keep us locked into thinking and feeling patterns that inhibit the expression of soul. In Greek mythology and East Indian folklore, for example, the gods are playful creatures, and life is a stage on which they express the characteristics that are inherent in play: spontaneity, creativity, variety, fun. What adults often call play—eating, drinking, watching television—has none of these qualities. These passive activities even block soul development with their potential for addiction and their training in passivity.

We learn only to fill ourselves up and watch the world go by.

Play—real, soul-inspiring play—means engaging in life and connecting with people in a positive, even exciting way. After playing we feel full of life, relaxed and less inhibited, and filled with a kind of empowering good feeling or even love. Although this sounds like the same sort of feeling that could be inspired by three drinks at a cocktail party, it is not. The feeling brought on by the three drinks wears off, requiring another three drinks and another, and eventually we get not happiness, but despair; if these good feelings are not self-generating. If we need a substance to experience them, then we don't know how to get there on our own, but need to rely on an induced chemical experience.

These feelings are potential for all of us, no matter how much we have obscured them. In my work over the last 20 years using drama games and experiential forms of therapy, I continue to be impressed at the depth of release of pent-up emotions that happens spontaneously through structured experiential exercises. Eventually, the suppressed ability to play finds its way to the surface and people can once again reclaim what is theirs, filling themselves with the regenerative powers of play, opening the door once again to that timeless world of the soul.

Play can also be perceived as a process that helps us gain mastery over inner struggles. Psychoanalyst Christopher Bollas said, "An individual may . . . struggle with traumatic inner constellations, and, by transformation of the trauma into works of art, achieve a certain mastery over the effect of trauma." Einstein believed "combinatory play [to be] the essential feature in productive thought—before there is any connection with logical construction and words or other kinds of signs which can be communicated to others." The underlying thesis here is that combinatory play leads to the "eventual establishment of a new perspective," says Bollas.

This reach toward symbolism and metaphor is a reach toward self and soul. Picasso called metaphor "a lie that tells the truth." We seek to describe our inner truths through this process. We are allowing ourselves inner space in which to "play" with issues, ideas and concerns related to the self in order to transform them and gain a shift in perception, a different perspective. Each of us in this sense has the capacity to be an artist, not because we will eventually produce a product that we wish to market, but because we are willing to take a journey inwards—to stay within the garden, the soil of the self, long enough, well enough, with enough care and focus, so that new life will sprout from old. Beauty might come from ugliness, and art from the ordinary.

This kind of play can provide a direct link with our own unconscious and inner self. It is tremendously useful in learning to access and make friends with the self and give expression to the voice of soul.

❦

To play is to be unfettered and unconditioned, to perform actions that are intrinsically satisfying: to sing, dance, and laugh . . . As players, then the gods are revealed to be delightful, joyful, graceful beings whose actions are completely spontaneous, unconditioned, and expressive of their transcendent completeness and freedom.

David R. Kinsley, *The Sword and the Flute*

CREATIVITY

Helped are those who create anything at all, for they shall relive the thrill of their own conception, and realize a partnership in the creation of the Universe that keeps them responsible and cheerful.

Alice Walker, *The Temple of My Familiar*

Twenty-five years ago, I went to an art school as a drama student. The competition to be perceived as creative and talented was intense. At my school we were all concerned with matters of art. We considered ourselves the elite and the highly creative. However, after a year or two, I realized that this very identity could become deadening and inhibiting. To be an artist is a day-to-day experience that has no name. It is a process, a point of view, a way of seeing the world.

Shortly after I graduated, I met my husband. I will never forget watching him arrange a bookshelf in our first house. He took time to arrange and rearrange it, each time glancing at it, looking, studying to see if he liked this way or that. I went through a long internal process as I watched.

At first I wondered why he spent so much time on a task that I rated unimportant. I felt that I knew, after several years of art school, what was important and creative, and arranging a bookshelf did not fall into that category. Gradually, however, I could not help but notice the joy he was taking in exercising his aesthetic eye and the pleasure and satisfaction that he was experiencing.

My next thought was a sort of dumbfounded admiration, almost an awakening. This was what I had been looking for all those years in art school. His arranging was creativity in action in a place where it meant absolutely the most: in a little corner of our home, where we would pass by and enjoy it. He was sharing himself with his personal environment and making it pleasing and expressive of his own taste and point of view.

Suddenly everything that seemed erudite in art faded away, and the woodenness and arrogance that I had also come to feel seemed completely understandable. Of course! We become wooden and arrogant and detached if we categorize and label some experiences as creative and others as banal and not worth attention. Creativity cannot be bought and sold. It cannot be packaged. It is the act of giving, the willingness of being with, exploring, trying different ways. It is simplicity itself. And when it seeks to be otherwise, it loses some of its ability to communicate.

When we watch children make a castle in the sand or draw a picture, we are watching creativity in action. Observe how their every movement seems devoted to the task at hand and how fully engaged they are with all of their senses in what they are doing. Their concentration is so deep that they find interruption jarring. They wish only to be left free to pursue this most satisfying activity, which has put them in touch with their own spontaneity and allowed them to enter a space of deep nurturing and satisfaction.

Although we have chosen to designate a certain corner of our society as artistic, relegating this characteristic to a particular sector of individuals and disowning it in ourselves, there is absolutely no reason why we can't each discover the artist within us and allow that artist fuller expression in our lives. Creativity is a state of mind, a place within from which we can bring forth those parts of ourselves that are spontaneous and original. In the moments of actual creation, the intellect is quiet. The observing ego has its hands quietly folded in its lap, while the creative aspects of the person are warmed up and engaged in the task at hand. The inner judge takes a recess.

Maria Montessori talks about periods of concentration experienced by children. She observed that if children are allowed the freedom to focus on a particular project or activity and given all the time and space that they wish, their subsequent periods of concentration will be deeper and longer. This allows them to go into a state that results in active involvement and deep concentration. When children learn to do this, they become more comfortable with this state of internalized mind. In a sense it becomes a sort of discipline. As adults we can cultivate this state in a very similar manner by giving ourselves the time and space and the lack of interruption to move into deeper states of mind that are creative and nourishing.

When we do this on a fairly regular basis, we can move into this state more easily in day-to-day situations, and we can take this meditative focus even into ordinary everyday experiences—cooking, reading, banking, cleaning. The more we will encourage our soul to express its uniqueness and joy in the world, the more we live soulfully in ordinary life.

✹

Every art requires the whole person.

French proverb

DOWNTIME

In the nineteenth century the problem was that God is dead; in the twentieth century the problem is that man is dead. In the nineteenth century inhumanity meant cruelty; in the twentieth century, it means schizoid self-alienation. The danger of the past was that men became slaves. The danger of the future is that men may become robots.

Erich Fromm

We live in a culture that paces itself to the speed of machines. We are trying like good little robots to match our speed with theirs. Humans cannot move at the same rate as machines. When we attempt to, we lose contact with our own humanness. We have forgotten who is master. The machines we have made should be here to serve us, not enslave us. We have made such super machines that we have come to feel inadequate next to them, but what machine could write a poem or admire a bird in flight, or kiss a lover on a sunny day? What machine could cradle a child or laugh or cry?

Humanness is our most valuable possession, and our window to soul. When we model ourselves after machines rather than people, we organize our lives as if we had no need for rest. But no one can be up all the time without paying a price for it. We need downtime, time to do nothing, to listen to the wind, to feel the sun's warmth on our faces. Many people are frightened by blank space on a calendar, but it is this very blank space that enriches our relationship with soul and, consequently, with everyday life. The meaning of life reveals itself to us in downtime. When we over-schedule ourselves, keeping ourselves in a state of outwardly focused activity, we deny ourselves time to process experience.

Life is a balance. We need active and passive time, periods of time in which we are engaged in activity and periods of times in which the mind can process that activity. Without process time, we are unable to integrate experience, to come to understand its particular meaning to us and its relevance to our own lives. We all need time to just be. Over-scheduled children are being taught to avoid and fear time spent quietly on their own. They are being trained not to drop down within themselves in spontaneous contemplation, but to be constantly goal-focused. We need goals to help us organize our lives, but the trick in contented living is to have the right balance of goal-oriented and non-goal-oriented time; too much in either direction will produce anxiety and instability.

People become scattered and nervous when they do not have sufficient quiet. Being scattered and nervous can lead to deeper problems. Stress builds up over time and eventually wears down our emotional and biological systems. When this happens, we do not have resistance either to physical illness or emotional events impinging on us. We lose our perspective and our center. Anything, physical or emotional, has the ability to rock us and throw us off balance.

When we can give ourselves enough time to allow our process of integration to take place without interruption, we come in touch with our own uniqueness and soul energy. Soul is present always, but we are too busy to notice. Downtime allows the soul to rise to the surface, like cream, to enrich our lives.

✺

*Only in solitude do we find ourselves, and in finding
ourselves, we find in ourselves all our brothers in solitude.*

Miguel De Unamuro

A LITTLE MADNESS

*Damnit boss, I like you too much not to tell you. You've got everything . . . every-
thing but a little madness. A man needs a little madness, otherwise he will always be
afraid to cut the ropes and truly be free.*

Nikos Kazantzakis, *Zorba the Greek*

The dances and songs of ancient cultures are ways to express "a
little madness," to release in us that which longs for expression. Each
of us needs to find a voice and an expression for that part of ourself,
to remove the gag that chokes us and keeps us from taking the risk
of self-expression. Allowing ourselves to be free is allowing the side
of ourselves that we fear might be ridiculed and rejected to find some
form of expression.

We need a little madness. We need for a moment to be able to
spurn the good opinion of others to allow our innermost selves to come out.
If we edit every thought or feeling, trim it around the edges, box it and shrink-wrap it to make it presentable, we will not be able to let our creative juices

**When we remember we are
all mad, the mysteries disappear and life stands
explained.**

Mark Twain

flow. Growth is messy. Real self-expression is spontaneous. Bind it
and we bind our soul along with it. Set it free and we give our spirit the opportunity to take flight. Implicit in this is a kind of honesty.

Allowing hidden parts of ourselves to come forth before we change them into what we would like them to be requires us to sit with and look at all of who we are. This deepens our humanness, our ability to accept our humanness and our ability to embrace the humanness of others.

We need to seek out actively situations that encourage this expression of soul, to find somewhere to be crazy, to access the demons we fear within us so that we can bring them forward for a moment into the arena of self and integrate them. When we cast them out, the out they are thrown into is our own unconscious. When we pretend that they are not there, we cannot integrate them into our own concept of who we are. When we cannot integrate them into the concept of who we are, they rule us and dictate our actions without our knowing it. We pass them on in insidious ways to those around us. We take rigid, locked positions hoping that if we are immovable, they will not leak out or penetrate our beings. Alas, they do.

Without a little madness, those aspects we have that are incongruous with and an insult to our good self-image are too painful to accept. Perhaps it is a little madness that will allow us to have parts of ourselves that are far from perfect. Not at all what we wish they were, but part of us nonetheless. When we can allow them to be a part of us and integrate them into our self-concept, they lose their destructive power.

A little madness allows us to take a flying leap into our own souls, to dare to believe that there is a force of soul with which we are and can be in beautiful alignment, to risk seeing soul in all that surrounds us. Perhaps it is mad to think that the world is fundamentally the stuff of soul, but is there a good enough reason to think otherwise?

If you don't crack the shell, you can't eat the nut.

Persian proverb

BONDING WITH THE SOUL

IF I WERE AN ANIMAL

Reflection: Sit comfortably and imagine, or write in your journal, answers to the following questions:

- ❦ If I were an animal, I would be _____.

- ❦ The qualities I admire most in my animal are_____.

- ❦ The drawbacks of this animal might be _____.

- ❦ The strengths of my animal are _____.

- ❦ If my animal could talk, she would say _____.

- ❦ My animal's favorite activity is _____.

- ❦ My animal hates to _____.

- ❦ My animal would like to be perceived as _____.

- ❦ Never call this animal _____.

Journal: Write a journal entry speaking as this animal—a soliloquy or monologue in the first person, as if your animal was writing her autobiography.

BONDING WITH THE SOUL

LIFE STRESSES

Reflection: Sit quietly and allow yourself to imagine and feel the various stresses in your life. Answer these questions in your mind or journal.

- 🐚 How do you react to stresses? Do you try to flee from thinking about them, or do you compulsively categorize and manage the thoughts?

- 🐚 Where in your body do you feel tension or carry your stresses?

Journal: In your journal, list the stresses. Next to each stress, write a rating from 1 to 10, 10 being the most stressful. Next, choose one of the stresses and write it in the middle of the page and draw a circle around it. Using triangles to represent males, circles to represent females and squares to represent non-human elements, locate yourself on the page wherever it feels right. Then locate symbols representing other people and elemnets of the stressful situation in relationship to you. In other words, if they are large and far away, make them large and far away. If they are small and close, make them small and close.

- 🐚 What do you see about your stress chart that surprises you?

- 🐚 What can you learn about how you handle or perceive stress from your chart?

- 🐚 Which aspects of your chart raise the most anxiety?

- 🐚 Which aspects do you feel hopeless about?

- 🐚 Which aspects do you feel stubborn about?

- 🐚 What changes can you make in your living patterns to reduce stress?

11
Universe

THE BIG BANG THEORY

*He on whom the sky, the earth, and the atmosphere
Are woven, and the wind, together with all life-breaths,
Him alone knows the one Soul.*

Mundaka Upanishad

Modern science is rediscovering soul at the heart of the universe. The origin of the universe is the origin of space, time, matter and energy. All physical things had their source from a single event, a sequential unfolding.

Anglican theologian Rowan Williams speaks of the Big Bang theory not as an explosion that created everything instantly, but as a story of time moving forward, unfolding, much like the Biblical allegory of the seven days of creation. In this single creative event we find the origin of all material things—mountains, rivers, deserts, dragonflies, Gila monsters, horses, people. When we speak of one source for all things, one energy out of which all else has come, we describe soul.

We are also concurring with the Biblical story of creation, the story of Genesis, this one soul energy from which all life springs. All of what we are—our physical energy toward movement, feeling, being, perception—has its origin in this singular energy event. All that is comes from one source. The birth of the universe is the energy upon which we live.

*For the soul is the beginning of all things.
It is the soul that lends all things movement.*

Plotinus

Physicist Stephen Hawking speaks of the universe as having no external creator; rather *the force of creation is intrinsic in all that is*. He feels space and time might be without boundaries, that the universe has no beginning or ending. How like the eternity that saints and sages have spoken of for centuries that sounds. It seems natural that when we are in meditation or stillness, our psyches would go toward something that we are in touch with that has no beginning and no ending. Something we have called eternity. In a way, we are just coming in touch with our own origins.

❦

We all live in and are made of a sea of neurons alive and in motion at all times. We are crossing into unknown regions of understanding. We are going into the very small and the very large and to our surprise, the study of the very large and the study of the very small are the same thing. If one wants to attach religious significance to that, I think one can. That decision is for each person to make . . . but what we can say scientifically is that the early universe had a symmetry to it, a beauty to it, and that creation in the sense of space and time as we know it did come into existence at an epoch fifteen billion years ago. I get very excited that I'm living at this time when human beings are first able to start to learn something about the universe that they can have confidence in, that they can have checked with experiment. No previous generation has had that opportunity. We're in that special time.

David Schramm, particle physicist
from *Soul of the Universe*

SOMETHING FROM NOTHING

In addition to souls which run and shriek and devour, might there not be souls which bloom in stillness, exhale fragrance and satisfy their thirst with dew and their impulses by their burgeoning?

Peter Tompkins and Christopher Bird

Try as they will, scientists cannot come up with an explanation for what might have caused the Big Bang. (Indeed, they can't agree that there even was a Big Bang.) The explosion was so intense that nothing is left from a previous time that could tell us what went before, if anything. Thus, the sudden expansion of space cannot be explained by traditional laws of physics. There needs to be another science that allows for the fact that *something* has sprung from *nothing* in order to describe our being here, our world, our age.

Scientists believe that quantum mechanics may provide that answer. It includes the worlds that govern the inner world of the atom, and it does not hold the view that the world operates only by cause and effect. Rather, it sees the world as operating through probabilities.

Quantum physics gives us a universe that is not predetermined. When it speaks of an evolutionary pattern that is governed by *probabilities*, it creates a true freedom. A quantum realm is ever alive and teeming with activity and creation. Things come into existence momentarily out of the quantum vacuum and then disappear again, over and over and over. According to Danah Zohar–physicist, philosopher and author of *The Quantum Self*—the

Before the revelations of the soul, Time and Space and Nature shrink away.

Ralph Waldo Emerson

quantum vacuum "is the underlying reality of all that is and everything that exists including ourselves, this chair, this glass. . . . It's as though there is a God, a sort of unrealized, unbroken wholeness . . . which is trying to realize itself through these excitations, through these disturbances of its own equanimity."

Nothing stands outside of nature, everything is a part of everything else. The scientific boundary between subject and object disappears in quantum physics. Viewing the universe in this way allows a scientific rationale for what many of us already know: that we are one with all that is, that we are connected with all things that are alive. It gives us a place in the scheme of things. It allows us to imagine that we, too, might come forth, be alive and fade away, as any other particle. The universe is inherently creative, always attempting to come forward and be made manifest in a variety of forms. When we come forth and when we fade away, we move from and into more of life. The inner and the outer become one.

The anthropic principle says that we as humans are a part of the universe, which in turn is uniquely designed to help us evolve, to aid in the evolution of the human mind. Theologian Rowan Williams said, "I think above all what I welcome is the sense that the mind is not just something existing in a vacuum playing on neutral items and trying to put them together into a theory, but the mind itself belongs in things; it responds to what's there and vibrates in tune. One of the things the anthropic principle says is: This is a universe in which mind belongs; it is a natural part of the system."

🔥

Earth's crammed with heaven,
And every common bush afire with God.

Elizabeth Barrett Browning

BONDING WITH THE SOUL

A Letter to God

Reflection: Close your eyes and allow yourself to dwell on God, on soul. Observe whatever comes up that keeps you from being totally present with a higher power. What disillusionment or disappointment might you have experienced toward a higher power, or what anger and resentment might you carry? How does it feel to attempt to sit in the presence of your own spiritual nature and what does that bring up within you?

Journal: Write a letter to God, beginning with, "Dear God," and closing any way that feels appropriate. Let God know not only what you are thankful for, but where you are disappointed. Let God see your anger as well as your love, your strength as well as your weakness. Say any and all that is on your heart that needs to be spoken in order to clear and deepen your intimate relationship with your higher power.

12
Spirituality

PERSONAL RELATIONSHIP WITH GOD

If there were no God, I would feel a need to create one.

Jean Jacques Rousseau

When a friend asked a priest if there was a God, he turned to her and replied, "Does it matter?" To my way of thinking, this is the most real and centered response to a question that ultimately needs to be experienced rather than answered. What does it really matter if there is no self as the Buddhists believe, or an essential self, as in Vedanta philosophy? What does it really matter if there is a God to which people can testify, or if there is not one to which people can testify?

If we need the assurance that there is a God in order to have faith in our hearts, then we have lost the battle before we have begun. The only real knowingness comes to us from what the yogis have called direct experience, which is what Psalm 46 means by, "Be still and know that I am God." When

> *The finding of God is the coming to one's own self.*
>
> Meher Baba

we enter a meditative state, we realize that these questions are already being answered and begin to seem irrelevant, that they are the intellect's way of throwing up a barrier between ourselves and experience.

In a search for God, soul and self, we always end up coming home, like Dorothy in *The Wizard of Oz*. When asked by Glinda, the Good Witch, what she learned on her journey, she replied, "I learned that if I ever lose my heart's desire again, I won't go looking past my own backyard because if it isn't there, I never really lost it to begin with." Dorothy's search for the wizard who would solve her problems ended in the discovery that the wizard to whom she assigned magical powers was himself only a man behind a curtain with all the needs and frailties that she, herself, had.

We can make the journey endless by seeking God or self outside of ourselves, in people, places and things, or we can shorten it by turning inward and looking for God where God is most likely to be.

§

Search yourself, and you will find Allah.

Kurdish proverb

THE MODERN MYSTIC

What about the awe you felt when your child was born, when you first made love or with the starry night, what about the awe astronauts have experienced on the moon. They all came back mystics. Their souls changed up there. You see the opposite of awe is taking it all for granted and our civilization has been taking it for granted for a long time. That's one reason why we're bored and we're violent and we don't have reverence and, therefore, a sense of the sacred toward the soil, the waters and the air.

Matthew Fox

Most people think of mystics as little men in long robes, or small women with beatific smiles. They almost always live in a land far, far away, sit on mountains or live in caves, and devote their lives to the attainment of esoteric knowledge that most of us never touch. But typically, this is not the case. Just as you have better access to your own internal healer and wise person than anyone else, you are also your own greatest mystery. Searching within allows each of us to be a modern mystic.

There is no need to find a place better than where you are to embark on your own inner development. The key is how you experience where you are, and how you use where you are to deepen the self. If you build a path toward self and soul, self and soul will certainly come forth. Out of your own shadowy depths, your own darkness, *you* will emerge.

For modern mystics, transformation may come less from harsh discipline, denial and self-abnegation, and more from the gentle discipline of surrender and observation. This kind of discipline arises out of the awareness that we are fundamentally interconnected. Once we are willing to know and be conscious of the effect of our actions, both on ourselves and those around us, we know that to hurt ourselves is to hurt another and to hurt another is to hurt ourselves. In our withdrawal from self, we feel lonely and forget that to connect with another we need to remain connected with the self.

Loneliness and self-alienation are maladies of our times. The privileges of affluence as a culture and the mobility of contemporary life are both enriching and isolating. Our struggle now seems to be toward humanness and spirituality as a way to cope with living in a world that is shrinking daily through improved communications, and a country where the average person will move 7.2 times. Our responses range from running from the pain of alienation from self and others, to somehow finding a way to expand within to include it all.

Psychology and mysticism are disciplines that are meant to marry. One without the other can be incomplete, though either path thoroughly examined contains the seeds of the other within it. Psychology helps us learn how to make conscious our own emotional blocks, barriers and issues so that we can work to resolve them. Once we have resolved our basic emotional issues, we need to go beyond our search for self in past circumstances to become fully self-actualized.

The spiritual path offers an extension of our search for self. One mistake seekers on the spiritual path make is to skip over emotional issues and adopt spiritual attitudes. But this is not a path of attitudes; it is a path of being, and entering it with anything less than our whole being will not augur well for our success on it. If we do not face our emotional issues, they will block us from our soul or spiritual selves and all the best attitudes in the world will only be partial solutions. We need to face ourselves fully as we are in order to get closer to our spiritual or soul natures, to clear out the debris, the baggage and the distortion that clouds our inner vision.

Modern mystics, having witnessed their own inner transformation, know that change comes from within. They also understand that when enough people choose to turn within for answers, or for peace of mind, instead of madly seeking it outside the self, they will also experience an inner transformation. And when enough people do this, the world, too, will be transformed.

*

Normal life is compatible with supreme realization and . . . direct mystical contact with the Divine can be sustained in any setting or activity. This is a revolution, for it dissolves all dogmas and hierarchies, all separations between ordinary and spiritual life, sacred and profane, humdrum and mystical. A new spiritual age has dawned for humankind, an age in which the Divine will be present intimately, normally, consciously in all things and activities. . . .

Andrew Harvey

SELF-ACTUALIZATION AND PEAK EXPERIENCE

1. *Self-actualizers are more efficient perceivers of reality and have more comfortable relations with reality.*
2. *They have an acceptance of themselves, of others, and of nature rather than an inclination to vilify others and mistrust human nature.*
3. *They are more spontaneous in their actions and reactions, which embodies a kind of simplicity and naturalness.*
4. *They are problem centered in that they have tasks to which they devote themselves and can lose themselves in these tasks.*
5. *They have a need for privacy and detachment. From time to time they need some time alone.*

6. *They have a kind of autonomy and independence that enables them to be a part of their culture, but at the same time to stand apart from it and view it for exactly what it is worth.*

7. *There is a continued freshness of appreciation.*

8. *They have a high social interest.*

9. *They are creative.*

10. *They have an unhostile sense of humor.*

11. *There is a democratic character structure.*

12. *They have an ability to discriminate between means and ends.*

Abraham Maslow

Psychologist Abraham Maslow felt that optimally-functioning people, self-actualized people, were ordinary people who were aided in their development by peak experiences of joy, ecstasy and insight, similar in many ways to the mystical experience.

Mystics of every tradition speak of a spontaneous experience of God-consciousness, a seeing of true reality, in which our illusions of reality are replaced by a deeper vision of what *is*. Today this experience seems no longer to be confined to devout mystics. According to recent Gallup polls, four out of ten people in the United States and five out of ten in Great Britain report having had some sort of mystical experience.

As more and more ordinary people are reporting similar breakthroughs—perhaps as a result of therapeutic experiences such as retreats or 12-Step programs, Native American vision quests and the reawakening of interest in Eastern forms of spirituality that involve meditation practice—it seems that a next stage in psychology may be spirituality. According to Maslow, optimally-functioning people are aided in their development by peak experiences. With the aid of peak experiences, the normally functioning person can begin to move along the

Make no more giants, God! But elevate the human race at once!

Robert Browning

path to self-actualization. Self-actualized people have their own personal experience with spirituality. They are in touch with what we call here the experience of soul.

Rabbi Samuel Drexel explains some of the psychospiritual reorganization of a mystical or soul-aware view of life in day-to-day living.

If one considers oneself or one's life as a wheel in which there are spokes and then there is a central hub, then in the life without the divine, the ego is that hub, and all the spokes—the relationships and the events that happen—are important or unimportant insofar as they affect the ego. We're hurt, we're angry, we act. If one lives in the divine presence and displaces at the hub, his ego for God or for the Divine, then what happens to him is now related to that hub.

To live with soul awareness at the center of our consciousness is to transform the process of how we value life. Because soul is a central point of reference, issues are referred back to a center that contains soul consciousness.

Soul is an *experience*. We cannot think or reason our way into soul awareness. It requires a willingness on our part to take a leap of faith, suspend our disbelief and let go all of the preconceptions that obscure our vision. Then perhaps an inner door will open, through which we can walk into the world refreshed and whole.

ᘯ

We see only the outer covering of reality
and it's only when our inner senses are opened,
when our inner life is opened,
that we pierce through the unreality.

Sister Pascaline Coff

DIRECT EXPERIENCE

Life is a succession of lessons which must be lived in order to be understood.

Ralph Waldo Emerson

I recall being on a Labor Day picnic in the country when our children were small. Below our picnic area was a deep and beautiful ravine with a waterfall, where the children were playing. A couple of

Do not, I beg you, look for anything behind phenomena.
They are their own experience.

Diogenes

us heard one of the children scream and went sailing down the side of the ravine in seconds to see what might be the problem. When we got there, we realized that they were just playing. The children began to show me all of the beautiful rocks and trickles of water as the sunlight streamed down upon us all, making the children look like little gods at play. Because it was such an unusual situation, I found myself going along with them and entered irresistibly into their soulful playfulness. I do not know when I have had as much fun as I had that day romping through a ravine with nine- and ten-year-olds. I felt one with all that surrounded us. The adults on the hill above faded into the distance and all that was, remained that moment in the sun.

The picnic was breaking up by the time I returned. All of my grownup friends were going through the motions of gathering blankets and food and returning to civilization. I did not even attempt to describe where I had just been, though I think some of them knew. I was aghast at the realization that these children had this experience regularly and that this is what they meant when they said they wanted to *play*. Now I realized that when they played they entered into a new world of meaning and wonder and connection, that this was an arena where all bets from the real world were off and where only what was part of the interplay of the moment counted.

Soul carries on a wordless conversation with the life's mystery, and its greatest strength is in what the yogis would call *direct experience*. Children move in and out of this space with ease. When we have *direct experience*, we can let go of our compulsive need for information in an effort to pacify the ever-present question, Why am I here and what is life all about? We can come in touch with that part of ourselves that can *experience* what it is all about. Rather than take anyone's word for the belief that soul exists, we should rely on our own experiment with contacting it. We can connect with that which is eternal within us.

❦

> *Hence in a season of calm weather*
> *Though inland far we be*
> *Our souls have sight of that immortal sea*
> *Which brought us hither,*
> *Can in a moment travel thither,*
> *And see the children sport upon the shore,*
> *And hear the mighty waters rolling evermore.*

> William Wordsworth, "Intimations of Immortality
> from Recollections of Early Childhood"

BONDING WITH THE SOUL

THE INNER TEACHER

Reflection: Allow yourself to sit or lie in a comfortable position. Go to your breath and let even breathing lead you to your center. Imagine a quiet, peaceful place. See walking toward you a teacher.

- What does this teacher look like?

- How does this person walk?

- Picture your teacher coming into view and then gradually sitting down and facing you.

- Feel the presence of your inner teacher.

Journal: In your mind or in your journal, reverse roles with your inner teacher. As the teacher, talk to yourself. Tell yourself what you want yourself to know and to see at this moment. Reverse roles again and, as yourself, contemplate or read what your inner teacher has told you. Repeat as often as you wish.

BONDING WITH THE SOUL

PEAK EXPERIENCE

Reflection: Find a quiet and comfortable moment, close your eyes and try to identify a time when you felt that you had a peak experience. For example: becoming a parent, a professional experience, a relationship that changed your life and perspective, a course of learning that altered your life significantly, a brush with death, a spiritual experience or anything that caused a significant shift in perception or a paradigm shift in the way you perceive life. Bring the circumstance to mind fully so you can identify its influence in your life.

Journal: Respond to these statements:

My peak experience was _____.

It affected my thinking in these ways _____.

It changed my life like this _____.

It affected my view or self-concept in these ways _____.

I will never be the same in these ways _____.

The life lessons I have integrated from my experience are

_____.

13
Living
with
Soul

ENTERING THE STATE OF EMPTINESS

You do not leave your room. Remain sitting at your table and listen. Do not even listen, simply wait. Do not even wait. Be quite still and solitary. The world will freely offer itself to you to be unmasked, it has no choice, and it will roll in ecstasy at your feet.

Franz Kafka

Most of us, at some point in our lives, experience a sort of emptiness within us. We may describe it as a hole or a void or even as a feeling of depression or meaninglessness. Most people want answers. They want to ask the right question of the right person who will tell them the right answer that will rid them of emptiness forever. As a therapist I have to watch people struggle as they realize that there is no one answer, no label for a particular syndrome that will lead to a lasting cure of the gnawing feeling that they carry inside.

Paradoxically, the first step toward understanding the emptiness is to let go of the desperate need for an answer and instead accept and *enter* into it. Then simply embrace it, be with it, know it, feel its dimensions, describe it, learn about it and embrace it as a part of your inner world, a deep inner space within the self.

Eventually, instead of becoming more fearful of the emptiness, we will begin to feel more centered, more grounded. This is because so much of neurotic, pathological or obsessive-compulsive behaviors are an attempt to run from what we fear within ourselves. When we can walk toward what we have previously run away from, we walk through the fear to confidence.

As we experience our emptiness, it evolves, transforms and dissolves into other states in a continuing process. And if we remain there long enough, we may discover that this space is, in fact, not empty, but filled by the presence of soul.

❦

Teach me to care and not to care. Teach me to be still.

T. S. Eliot

PERCHANCE TO DREAM

The dream is that small hidden door in the deepest and most intimate sanctum of the soul, which opens into that primeval cosmic night that was soul long before there was a conscious ego and will be soul far beyond what a conscious ego could ever reach.

Carl Jung

When we read our dreams, we are reading our personal journal, a passage in our autobiography, a letter to the self. The plot represents our own particular spin on life, our unique vision of the world and *how we experience within the self system* all that we have gone through in the process of living. No one can know the meaning of our dreams better than we because it is we who have assigned a particular meaning to a particular symbol or metaphor.

Studying our dreams can be a profoundly rich source of soul knowledge because the language of dreams issues from the soul, from the imagistic and symbol-forming aspects of mind that connect us to our deeper selves and to the collective unconscious. Our deepest dreams allow us to come closer to parts of ourselves that we might otherwise be too preoccupied to notice, helping us to crystallize through symbol and metaphor what in the waking state may feel like a run-on sentence. Dreams speak to us. Learning to listen and interpret the language of our own dreams can give us an open channel of communication with our unconscious and strengthen our relationship with soul.

According to physicist and author Fred Alan Wolf, "Conscious awareness is not only consciousness of the outside world but also its representations in the brain. If so, the dream consciousness is definitely an altered state, a very interesting alteration indeed, in which the focus of awareness is internal representations and not outside ones." Our dreams reflect back to us *our particular view of reality,* organized from the data we collect, neatly coded and filed according to where it best connected or related to our highly personalized inner database. Dreams elucidate the ways in which we have organized the meaning of life experiences. The various ways in which we perceive meaning are influenced by both our own consciousness as well as what Carl Jung calls the collective unconscious, so that our dreams are a distillation of our interpretation of many levels of awareness. We see, played out on the dream stage of our minds, our own unique vision of the world represented in symbol and metaphor. Our dreams are our symbolic representation of life as it affects us, our deeply intimate personal story.

What Happens in the Brain

The language of dreams is the language of the self. Dreams have played an important role in ancient and primitive societies and continue to do so in many parts of the world. They are seen as carrying mystical meaning from the soul. Our dreams are our self-portrait, our personalized soul story authored by and for us, carrying meaning that is shaped and defined by our own unconscious.

Unlike Freud who sought hidden meaning in dreams, J. Allen Hobson feels that the meaning of dreams is "transparent and revealed." The brain's use of symbol is to "condense a lot of meaning into a revelatory clear meaning. The symbol is not there to make things obscure; it is to carry more latent meaning with it." He also feels that discontinuity in dreams is most likely cerebrally driven, reflecting neurological or biological fluctuations rather than particular meaning. Thus, in interpreting our own dreams, it is important only to relate to what feels meaningful and not to read meaning into every scene change or discontinuity.

REM State

One interesting theory about what goes on in the rapid eye movement (REM) state is that it is a sort of inner cleansing, a ridding of the self system of unwanted oscillations. In the REM state, the mind scans itself for what it does not wish to keep, discarding it rapidly as it assesses its undesirability. It can be seen as a natural function of the mind, cleansing itself of what it feels it does not need or wish to keep. We all may have experienced this at one point or another when being jostled out of a deep dream. That feeling that we were just in the middle of examining something that we had managed to bring into focus in dream language, in a constellation of metaphors carrying a particular sort of congealed meaning—the meaning being most available to us, the dreamer. We are, at that moment, scanning our own psyche and able to see what we wish to keep and what is not for us. The meaning is revealing iself to us.

In psychodrama we use role-play to examine the meaning of dreams. Each character or symbol in the dream is seen as an aspect of the self. Then the dreamer reverses roles with each character and speaks back to herself. First we choose a person, empty chair or object to "play" the character or symbol, and the dreamer talks to it. In this way the dreamer can become for a moment each of her internal representations of self, so that she can explore the particular meaning of each symbol or form that the self has chosen to represent itself.

Carl Jung saw dreams as an attempt to compensate for undeveloped archetypes or unrealized aspects of the self. Jung's method of exploring dreams was the use of *amplification*. Dreamers are asked to amplify each element of the dream, identifying what it reminds them of. They are encouraged to stay with that particular element of the dream, fully amplifying its personal meaning, rather than using free association. In this way, the meaning of the mind's use of a particular archetype to the person can be explored.

Studies using content analysis devised by Calvin Hall, Ph.D., report that there is considerable congruence between what we dream about and our preoccupations in waking life. This is known as the *continuity principle*. "Dreams objectify that which is subjective. They visualize that which is invisible, they transform the abstract into the concrete. They come from the most archaic alcoves of the mind as well as from the peripheral levels of waking consciousness. Dreams are the kaleidoscope of the mind. . . ."

Throughout human history dreams have been used by cultures as varying as aboriginal tribes to modern Western society, to describe the contents of self and soul. Whether used to guide, divine or inform, dreams are seen as carrying message and meaning, as being a doorway into the unconscious, a pathway to and from what lies beyond our conscious grasp, a voice that speaks of the mystery of life, the majesty and power of soul.

❦

In the drowsy dark cave of the mind
Dreams build their nest with fragments
dropped from day's caravan.

Rabindranath Tagore

LETTING GO OF NEGATIVE ATTITUDES

*There is but one thing that cannot be taken away from us and that is our attitudes.
It is in the realm of our attitudes that we can shape our salvation.*

Viktor E. Frankl

Negative, defeatist attitudes will do more damage to our planet than pollution or acid rain. They are the smog of the soul. They allow each and every one espousing them to divide themselves from being responsible and positive in the here and now. Anyone who is truly in touch with the soul experience finds it hard to be negative for too long. Simply said, the universe is too magical, too full of mystery and metaphor, too alive with beauty to give up on. Soul is hope incarnate, quiet expectancy, fundamentally generous and loving. When we are truly in touch with soul we know we are creative and dynamic.

No matter how cynical you become, it's never enough to keep up.

Lily Tomlin

Soul is one with the physical universe. The physical universe is intrinsically creative, dynamic and spontaneous, so to be aligned with soul is to be aligned with personalized power. The personalized aspect of power is the "I" referent—ourselves. We are the center of our own experience. The life of the universe passes through and is made aware through the "I" experience. We co-create our lives through the matrix of life energy and "I" energy each minute, each day, each year.

We may feel insignificant, as if no matter what we do, we will never make a difference. But living closer to the ordinary soul gives us options and impacts on another level. Understanding that we live in an alive universe gives us both a power and a responsibility to ourselves and our world. According to *The Only Planet of Choice*, complied by Phyllis V. Schlemmer and Balden Jenkins,

There are three areas of activity in which we can contribute: in our actions, we can reduce our contribution to destruction through altering our consumption habits, our waste, our choices and our way of working; in our behavior, we can love ourselves more, and treat others as we would have them treat us; and in our inner life, we can visualize world solutions, work on ourselves to become clearer and more open and phase out negative beliefs such as the anticipation of catastrophe.

This is a recipe for a life worth living, one that turns around the hopeless, demoralizing feeling that there's nothing much we can do. It brings a new feeling of empowerment and effectiveness. To some extent, we have to choose to believe that what we do makes a difference and accept that the challenge for us is to experiment and demonstrate that it does. Seeing is believing. And believing is seeing.

The attitudes that we hold are powerful, dynamic and felt by those around us, often more powerfully than spoken words. Our attitudes shape our inner life, relationships and social worlds. Taking responsibility for the contents of our minds is a major step in soul ownership and allows us to take our first steps toward soul in action.

We can destroy ourselves by cynicism and delusion, just as effectively as bombs.

Kenneth Clark

LIVE THE LIFE YOU HAVE

Live your own life, for you will die your own death.

Latin proverb

At one point in our lives together, my husband, our children and I were part of a spiritual community. That experience taught me that we don't need a spiritual community in order to identify with soul. Although it is helpful to have such a body of people or a teacher to learn about the soul path, ultimately our individual ability to integrate our path is most important.

A spiritual community is prey to all of the issues of vanity and ego that exist in any community of people. People are, after all, just human, and anyone who claims to be more than human should probably be suspect. We are not looking to relinquish our humanness. We are looking to identify with a spiritual energy and bring it into our level of experience so that, ultimately, we can become more human than before. One does not need knowledge if one has experience. Believing in something is still one step away from experiencing it. The goal in identifying with soul is to bring the actual experience of soul or soulfulness into more and more of daily living.

We all seek answers that will make everything simple and ensure that we will be happy all the time. In our determined search we gather transitory solutions. Eventually we come to the same conclusion—that this new plan, this new system, this new belief is one more thing that isn't it after all. When we realize that the answer we seek doesn't exist, we may sink back into fundamental despair, returning to that awful, gnawing feeling that we are just a number after all, and nothing we can do to distinguish ourselves will offset the reoccurrence of this feeling.

Eventually, we may come to the simplest of answers: that we are better off living the life we have, and living it well; that a quiet, contented commitment will produce more joy, engagement and belonging than any philosophy or belief system can reveal. We won't find a final scheme with a definitive solution because all solutions are momentary; the moment is all we have. Perhaps knowing this is part of what enables us to appreciate the moment just for what it is, no more, no less. Somehow this mysterious world, where none of us know from where we came nor where we will go, is a perfect kind of mystery that can only reveal itself to us when we allow it to unfold on a minute-to-minute basis. When we try to think it through, systematize it or package it, we are just reducing it and in the process, losing it.

We are all philosophers at heart. We seek to solve the mystery of our lives, to find the answer to the questions of our being, and there to find happiness. But the more we accept that *we are the question*, the greater our chance of finding peace. Happiness is more present in the process of releasing ourselves into the question, than in insisting that the answer be found upon which we can build contentment. Contentment and happiness are fleeting experiences. They come and go. Seeking to find and hold them only ensures our frustration and sets us up for a continual sense of inadequacy because happiness cannot be *found*. It can't be held, but only experienced, and experience comes and goes. The evolutionary process of identification and differentiation is infinite, unending. Therefore, to reach a point of resolution or solution is to stagnate, and stagnation is death.

We look for structures against which to define ourselves. Some of us seek to define ourselves in terms of family systems, a spouse or nuclear family; some in terms of professional accomplishments; some in belief systems, spiritual or intellectual biases. Always seeking a way to establish presence against the experience of nothing, or value against the experience of something.

Because life is a mystery, we fear falling into a hole of nothingness. The hole we fear exists within each of us. The profound insecurity we feel at not knowing why we are here or who we are produces in us a tremendous need to create enormous systems of thinking and believing in order to explain our presence here on Earth. The fear that we come from nowhere and will go to nowhere presses for an explanation that transforms the nowhere into a somewhere.

How much of our driving need to be somebody is motivated by our gnawing fear of being nobody? After all, who are we if we aren't someone's daughter, someone's mother or accomplished at something? Perhaps in the quest to define and become a somebody, we could also learn to make friends with the nobody who lives within us. Until we learn to accept and even embrace this nobody, we will be afraid of our own shadow, the nothingness that awakes us in the middle of the night.

One way to become less afraid of insecurity is simply to live the life we have to the best of our ability. Somehow the deepest mysteries of being, whether they are mysterious or simple, seem to be present and interwoven in the events, circumstances and interchanges of energies that exist in this universe. We are life and we are surrounded by life. Cause and effect are interrelated.

On a basic level, we can see the influence of our behavior on others. Although we may not say anything in particular, others respond to our attitude—not to what we say, but to what we put into the emotional climate. Their reading of that emotional climate will have more influence on interactions than words. This is a sort of energy exchange that goes on all the time, over and over throughout the day. Each day calls upon us to be aware of the *affective* atmosphere, and how we contribute and react to that atmosphere.

The Buddhists tell us that fundamentally all is nothingness, and that our desire to create something so we can define ourselves against the nothing is the subtlest barrier to releasing fully into the moment. Vedanta philosophy tells us that there is an ultimate something against which all else has meaning. That something and energy is consciousness. That consciousness has been called God, love, eternity, that which is changeless. From this point of view, there is a something that does exist. In my opinion, ultimately it does not matter what one calls this something. If it is God, Love, Higher Self, Higher Consciousness or nothingness. What matters is accepting it as a living energy connecting all things.

All things are interrelated at a fundamental level by a consciousness or energy, and to align ourselves with this consciousness or God-energy is to come closer to a sense of self and soul. Living the day at hand can have a spiritual, mystical and transformative value. When we accept that the day before us has within it all of the deepest components of mystery, love and God that any moment of teaching or doctrine could contain, then to experience the moment directly is to experience the soul directly. To do otherwise, to distance ourselves from the moment, is to distance ourselves from the soul, because the soul is contained in the present moment.

It is not that the search is not fascinating or exciting or even enlivening. Only that there are no answers. At least, not based on intellectual belief systems. To seek the answers in those systems is simply to rearrange the question and find a partial answer. The experience of soul is the acceptance of the moment in which both the question and the answer dissolve and become irrelevant.

ꙮ

If I hadn't taken up painting, I would have raised chickens.

Grandma Moses

I-THOU vs. I-IT

The true opposite of love is not hate but indifference. Hate, bad as it is, at least treats the neighbor as a thou, whereas indifference turns the neighbor into an it, a thing.

Joseph Fletcher

The I-Thou relationship recognizes that all that surrounds us is a product of consciousness and, therefore, is alive to the same degree that we are alive. The I-It relationship says that only we are conscious and that all else is void of life or energy; all else is an it.

When we allow ourselves to see the world as a Thou rather than as an It, it comes to life in the palms of our hands, in the casual thought that we think, in the energy that we take to the task at hand, in the way in which we interact with people in the moment that surrounds us. When the world becomes a Thou, it has the same life that we feel we have, and there is a possibility for an exchange of energies between I and Thou, Thou and I, that allows us to feel held and nurtured by the very presence of life and spirit around us.

When we only see the world as an I-It relationship, we do not allow for the exchange of energy from object to self because we do not recognize that what is around us is as alive as we are. Seeing the world as an It invites loneliness and isolation in an artificial world in which everything surrounding us is lifeless and without spirit. This kind of isolation makes us feel as if we are alone in a void. It is a loveless place because love and spirit and energy and soul are interrelated, even one and the same, and it is our recognition of this soul energy or love energy—our acceptance of the I-Thou—that allows our energies and the energies around us to flow together, to intermingle.

Philosopher and theologian Martin Buber argued that in life things happen by chance and succeed. But as soon as we make openness and spontaneity a goal and pursue it as such, we are lost in the desire to control the outcome, which makes the actual outcome lifeless and prescripted. We live with the illusion that if we try hard enough, think hard enough, work hard enough and plan well enough, we will be able to control the outcome of a given situation. Soul tells us to *take the action and let go of the results.* When we feel that we can control the outcome, we live in the result rather than the process. Trying to control results dams the waters within us, and we spend our energy on managing rather than living. When we feel that we are somehow responsible for the outcome, we get tangled in a tedious maze of micro-management in which we attempt to determine, then manipulate, other people's feelings, perceptions and actions.

For example, say your goal is to have the perfect vacation. As soon as this becomes your goal, the less alive and spontaneous your vacation is likely to be. The more you try to control "having a wonderful time," the more tense you become and the less likely it is that you will ever relax enough to enjoy yourself. It is a setup for disappointment if the vacation isn't perfect.

We have all had the experience of reaching a sought-after goal, only to be vaguely disappointed by the outcome. The process of seeking was more exciting and spontaneous than the attainment of the goal. What is it about the process that is more alive than the capturing of the goal? The key is that although usually we define the goal in great detail, we do not define every moment of how we will achieve it. This leaves more room for chance and spontaneity on the road to the goal than in reaching the goal itself.

So it is with our own lives. Living one day at a time allows us to recognize that we are not in charge of the blueprint. We are allowing spirit and chance and spontaneity to be a part of our day. We begin to experience our own aliveness in the world in which we live, the I-Thou relationship in action and feeling and thought.

❧

Most people ask for happiness on condition.
Happiness can only be felt if you don't set any condition.

Arthur Rubenstein

BONDING WITH THE SOUL

TURNING IT OVER

Reflection: Close your eyes and imagine how you would like to resolve a particular situation in your life that is bothering you. Allow yourself in your imagination to see, feel, taste and participate in the resolution as you would like to experience it.

Journal: Divide a piece of paper into three horizontal sections. In the bottom section, write a few phrases to describe the situation you want resolved as it is at present. In the top section, write a few phrases or sentences describing it as you imagined it resolved. Leave the middle space empty so that the divine hand of spirit or higher power has space to work.

BONDING WITH THE SOUL

LIVING WITH SOUL

Reflection: Allow a dream that you have had recently or one you remember to come to mind. Picture the dream moving before your inner vision; watch it, let it envelop you. Feel the atmosphere of the dream and let the characters, symbols or objects that stand out move into the foreground of your consciousness.

Journal: For each aspect of the dream—each person, element or important object—write an amplification. Clarify what each element represents or is trying to communicate. Speak as if you are the object or element. Write a brief first-person soliloquy, a proclamation, such as: "I am a star in a dark sky. I shine even when I cannot be seen." Amplify each object or person that feels significant and then continue to explore even those that seem pushed into the background as unimportant. When you have finished this process, answer these questions:

❦ Does one character or element seem to say the most or speak the loudest?

❦ Which element is it and what does it say to you?

❦ Why do you think you had this particular dream when you did?

❦ What was the dream trying to tell you?

BONDING WITH SOUL

LETTING GO OF NEGATIVE ATTITUDES

Reflection: Allow yourself to take a caring and intimate look within.

❧ Where are you insecure and where are your negative attitudes about yourself and how are they blocking your life?

❧ Where do these attitudes keep you preoccupied and hold you back?

Journal: Write your own affirmations. No one knows you as well as you. No one knows where you hurt as clearly as you, or knows what attitudes need changing. Write the affirmations that you need to hear to turn negative attitudes into positive ones. For example: Inner attitude: No matter how hard I try, I will always look dumpy. Affirmation: My beauty comes from within. I acknowledge and welcome the beautiful being within me. Each day I invite her to come forth in all ways.

Write affirmations regularly and repeat them to yourself throughout the day.

14
Tuning the Human Instrument

SOME TOOLS

Give a man a fish and you feed him for a day,
Teach him to fish and you feed him for a lifetime.

Chinese proverb

We live through this house of our body, mind and spirit. Rather than deny it, we need to learn to refine it, temper it, educate it, keep it clean and free from unnecessary debris. In this way the vehicle through which we live can be brought into balance. Real balance feels light and flexible. The discipline involved can be friendly and compassionate, with no need for force.

Just as we each have our own unique physical makeup, we each have our own psychological makeup. In dealing with physical disease we need to treat the cause rather than just repress the symptom. If we only repress the symptom, the underlying illness can undermine the body's immune system. I believe the mind also has a sort of immune system, and we have a natural ability to ward off psychological conditions that are discordant with our natural character. For example, use of controlling and repressive methods in child rearing to treat psychological symptoms can undermine or compromise our natural psychological immune system. The mind needs an appropriate balance of discipline and freedom to find its own unique way of being content and fulfilled. It needs the space and support to come to know and understand itself so that it can respond to its own particular needs.

Soul speaks through the body, the human instrument. If the instrument is out of tune, the melody—no matter how pure and clear it is at the outset—becomes distorted and out of tune. The techniques you will find in this section are not the usual step-by-step instructions toward enlightenment offered in self-help books. Rather, they are suggestions for some of the tools you can learn to use to help you live more spontaneously, creatively and in tune with the song of your true nature.

🌿

Begin to weave and God will give the thread.

German proverb

ASKING FOR HELP

To question a wise man is the beginning of wisdom.

German proverb

Asking for help clears the path toward soul. The psychological and emotional openness of asking for help humbles and opens us to new learning. Automatically it lowers our defenses, opening us to others and others to us.

The openness allows us the freedom to fail or succeed and to learn that failure is a part of a process, not the end of it. There is no shame in asking for assistance and bringing in other people, nor is failure permanent. We are also, then, free to succeed and to need more help even while being successful.

On a spiritual level, "Seek and you shall find, knock and the door shall be opened to you" describes an inner reaching toward something beyond the temporal experiences, the acknowledgment of forces beyond the illusion of reality. Asking for help on this level connects us with the quantum physical level, or the mind of God. It allows spirit to work in our lives.

🌿

I can't go on. You must go on. I'll go on.

Samuel Beckett

THE INNER TEACHER

Ultimately, our best teacher is ourselves.
When we are open, aware, and watchful,
then we can guide ourselves properly.

Tarthang Tulku

Over 20 years ago, I traveled to India. I found the Indian people extraordinarily cordial, kindly and human. One evening I was having dinner with some teachers. The gentlemen on my left was a doctor of philosophy, and by way of making dinner conversation, I asked him who his favorite philosopher was.

"You are," he replied.

I thought he had misunderstood me and so repeated the question. Again, he looked at me and said in perfect English, "You are."

Bewildered, I asked, "What do you mean by that?"

"No one knows you like you know yourself," he explained, "and no one can create a philosophy appropriate for your life as well as you can."

Accessing an inner teacher or a sense of inner guidance allows us to feel connected from within and helps us to balance voices that come from the outside.

To believe what is true for you in your heart is true for all men, that is genius.

Ralph Waldo Emerson

SIMPLICITY

Every creative act requires elimination and simplification. Simplification results from a realization of what is essential.

Hans Hoffmann

Simplicity, which enables us to quiet our lives, is at the center of any spiritual pursuit. One way to gain this simplicity is to practice what the yogis call "meditation in action." In meditation, when thoughts rise and demand our attention, we do not latch onto them and follow their complicated path, but allow them to pass by, simply observe them and let them go. In the same way, in living our lives, we should not latch onto every event that happens to us and complicate it beyond its original meaning, but experience it and let it go.

Practicing simplicity, as the phrase implies, is not always easy. We have spent our entire lives making things much more difficult, dramatic and fraught with meaning than they need to be. But we cannot see our soul if it is surrounded by our own manufactured complexities.

To accept the activities of the day without complicating them allows us to have a simple relationship with them. We gain perspective, seeing the affairs of our lives with different eyes so that they do not have the power to run us. Simplicity allows us to be with ourselves rather than to lose ourselves in every thought and action that passes through our minds. In this way it helps us to set inner boundaries. When our energy flows willy-nilly into every issue that enters our minds, the energy is no longer under our command but belongs to the thought or thing that has taken it over. Within the limitation of boundaries, our thoughts can settle peacefully, like a lake between mountains.

I have a simple philosophy. Fill what's empty.
Empty what's full. And scratch where it itches.

Alice Roosevelt Longworth

BECOMING AWARE OF EMOTIONAL TRIGGERING

Individual brain cells, after repeated exposure to similar events, begin to react in the same fashion each time: In other words, they learn. The human brain then starts to categorize and [to] group images, and then we use these complex sets to make abstractions. This process, created and reinforced in childhood, creates memories, which rarely go away. They may be hidden from the conscious mind, but they remain locked in the brain, waiting for a trigger to bring them to the surface.

Daniel Akron

Understanding triggering is a truly useful concept in learning how to work with our own personality. We all overreact to certain life circumstances. We sense that the depth and intensity of our reaction is more than appropriate, given what actually is happening. If we can step back from this reaction and try to see what unfinished business has caused the reaction, we can grow rather than act out.

The process is simple. Identify the overreaction, explore it and be open to experiencing the feelings underneath it. The feelings will probably stem from a situation that felt painful and unmanageable in the past. If it was never resolved, it lives in us as an unhealed wound, and when the wound is pressed, it still hurts. Rather than assume the hurt is caused by what is happening today, let yourself explore the possibility that part of the hurt, anger or uncomfortable feeling aroused belongs to prior events.

If you live in the river you should make friends with the crocodile.

Punjabi proverb

Let yourself feel it. As you do, a plethora of images will run through your mind and supply you with missing pieces of the puzzle. Through this process you can make appropriate connections as to the origins of your emotional reaction and begin to separate the past from the present. This way the present can be used as a vehicle for understanding the past, rather than the past infiltrating and contaminating present situations in unhelpful ways. When you do this, you can turn a potential crisis into a personal growth experience.

If you are distressed by anything external, the pain
is not due to the thing itself but to your own
estimate of it; and this you have the power to
revoke at any moment.

Marcus Aurelius

TURNING THOUGHTS OVER

If we did not worry, most of us would feel we were not alive. To be struggling with a
problem is for the majority of us an indication of existence. We cannot imagine life
without a problem; and the more we are occupied with a problem, the more alert we
think we are. . . . Will worry resolve the problem or does the answer . . . come when
the mind is quiet?

J. Krishnamurti

Anxiety is present when attachment to thought is present. When we have a thought that produces our anxiety, it is our particular *feeling* about that thought that makes us anxious. When we examine the thought more closely, we recognize that we have a choice as to how we respond to it. When we accept that we do not have the kind of total control of our life's events that we wish, we are able to let go a little.

Once we appreciate our essential powerlessness, we become empowered in a new way. Recognizing our powerlessness over life's vicissitudes allows us to establish an authentic alignment with real power. We see that the question is, "Can I do something about this, or can I not?" If the answer is "I can," we follow with an appropriate action. If the answer is "I cannot," then we can let it go, or turn it over to the loving hands of a higher power.

Events and stages in our lives have their season like every other living thing, and with their season will come sun after the storm. This is the natural pattern. To try to control the amount of rainfall is as pointless as to try to control many of life's events. We are part of nature, not above it or below it. When we take our rightful place within this context, we can learn to have a more tranquil life.

Most of our fears are irrational and will never be realized, but when one fear is realized, we feel we have justification for all of them. The more dull-witted elements of our minds always seek an object on which to focus in order to explain life, but this is no more reliable than to say the sun shines only on one tree and that the tree is the object of the sunshine. The sun is, in fact, impersonal, and the tree is one of many. The sun is not aiming at one particular tree any more than life's ups and downs target us. They happen because that is the nature of life.

Fear is built into us as a species. We can't help feeling fear, but we can help being controlled by it. When we have a thought that produces anxiety, examine the thought. The event will come and go whether or not we get upset. Recognize it and let it go without getting overly attached to the anxiety or fear it produces. Instead of turning the thought over and over in our minds, why not turn it over, in a spiritual sense, to a higher source? Although we may not be able to alter the anxiety-producing circumstance, we can alter our reaction, freeing ourselves from the anxiety-producing cycle in which we have been caught, and removing another obstacle from our path toward soul recognition.

And which of you by being anxious can add one cubit to the span of life? Consider the lilies of the field, how they grow; they neither toil nor spin; yet I tell you even Solomon in all his glory was not arrayed as one of these.

Matthew 6: 28-30

CONDITIONING AND SELF-DISCIPLINE

In this unbelievable universe in which we live there are no absolutes. Even parallel lines, reaching into infinity, meet somewhere yonder.

Pearl S. Buck

Mind is energy. To free mental energy so it is available for soulful living, we need to understand how our particular mind has been conditioned to think and to create meaning. One of the most valuable lessons I have learned throughout my professional life and training is that there is no one way to perceive anything. I used to feel torn between one way of doing therapy and another, one way of thinking and another. I am no longer bothered by conflicting theories and I try not to bother my clients with them or hold them to one path of healing. There is no one path, no one answer. Rather, there is your path, your answer. If we must reach some pre-conditioned idea of perfection before we start living, we will never get there, there is no starting or finishing. There is only continual flowing of the river of the mind.

We are in the best position to guide and discipline our minds when we recognize that force and control create a resistance in the mind. They are a last resort and tough to maintain. Steady, gentle guidance allows the mind to move in a general direction without force. It is the mind's nature to wander from one association to another. When it does this, gently call it back to the task at hand. Observe its wanderings and associations without getting lost in them.

Focusing in this way allows one to bring to attention what is being accomplished at the moment. It is not an act of force; rather, it is inviting the mind to attend in a gentle, natural manner. Rather than get derailed into them, observe the mind's meanderings as they happen, then call the mind back to the present.

Focusing enables you to bring not only conscious, but unconscious attention to the task at hand. It is as much the unconscious that creates distraction as the conscious.

Focusing works with the natural flow and power of the mind rather than against it. It allows for mental meandering, but then calls the mind back to the present. It enables one to accomplish a much greater amount because one's mental energy is not being dissipated and wasted through distraction.

Focusing trains the mind to penetrate the surface, which is what soul awareness is about—penetrating the illusory surface of life; moving toward a deeper reality and awareness.

❦

If I lose my direction, I have to look for the North
Star, and I go to the north.
That does not mean I expect to arrive at the North Star.
I just want to go in that direction.

Thich Nhat Hanh

CREATIVE VISUALIZATION

Visualization is the way we think. Before words, images were. . . . The human brain programs and self-programs through its images. Riding a bicycle, driving a car, learning to read, baking a cake, playing golf—all skills are acquired through the image-making process. Visualization is the ultimate consciousness tool.

Mike Samuels, M.D., and Nancy Samuels,
Seeing with the Mind's Eye

Creative visualization is the act of consciously picturing in our minds what we would like to experience in our lives. Whether it is good health, success or comfortable relationships, experiencing it first in imagination allows us to rehearse the experience over and over, and to prepare our minds to recognize and incorporate aspects of the experience when they occur. We change our "brain set," or what our brain is programmed to look for.

For example, if we believe we are lucky, we will perceive as good luck what others might see just as chance. That will add to our positive self-images, and cause us to be the kind of people who actively recognize and make the necessary moves and accommodations to build on that good fortune.

In our quest to experience ordinary soul, creative visualization can be an invaluable tool. By visualizing ourselves touching soul, we open the door to allow soul to come through.

Creative visualization is simple and pleasant to do. It is best done in quiet moments, such as first waking or when falling asleep, but it is also possible to visualize creatively as we go about our day-to-day tasks. The method for entering into a creative visualization is simple. First, focus on the situation that we want. Now allow it to come into our mind in its entirety. Picture it *happening*. Smell it, taste it, feel it, touch it, talk to it and listen to it talk to us, allow it to have color and movement. Interact with it as though it is really happening. Do this over and over again until we can see and feel ourselves in this situation, participating in it as if it were already a reality.

For creative visualization to manifest in life, become proactive; put yourself in life circumstances that will enable your dreams or visualizations to become actuality. Notice that serendipitous incidents issue from your creative visualizations. This is how our dreams become reality, how ordinary soul manifests in ordinary life.

This technique is useful on many levels. On the first and most primary level, it can help us create the mental reality that we want. It is a useful technique to employ in situations that intimidate or frighten us, even circumstances that we may be somewhat phobic about entering. We all have situations that make us uncomfortable, that can inhibit our easy passage through the world and keep us from doing things we'd like to do. If we can play these fears out mentally, by envisioning ourselves being comfortable in a situation that we dread, we begin to decondition our fear.

If even approaching the situation mentally provokes anxiety, we can approach it only to the point of anxiety. Breathe deeply, don't force it. Then allow yourself to picture just a little bit more. There is no rush. We can picture it repeatedly until we have a genuine feeling of comfort. Move just to the point of anxiety and then return to the breath and use it as a centering technique until little by little, the full situation and our participation in it comes into as full view as possible.

While we can creatively visualize for our own benefit, there is nothing wrong with doing the same thing for someone else that you care about. Use the same method. Picture the person you care about operating happily in a particular situation. This is a useful technique for parents to use with their children, and helps to reduce anxiety and diminish the kinds of behaviors that spring from parental anxiety toward the child. By visualizing the child well and happy with friends, feeling productive and included over and over and over again, we send this energy toward the child and also decondition our own anxiety. It also helps to control the subtle expectations we send our children.

It is also helpful to visualize a calm and tranquil life in which reaction and chaos are kept to a minimum, and we have space and time to breathe deeply and to commune with our soul. By creating the scene mentally, we are more likely to move toward it or create it actively.

🌱

Why should we be cowed by the name of action? Tis a trick of the senses no more. We know that the ancestor of every action is a thought. . . . to think is to act.

Ralph Waldo Emerson

WITNESS

We dis-identify by observing. Instead of being absorbed by sensations, feelings, desires, thoughts, we observe them objectively without judging them, without interfering with them in any way. We see them as distinct from us, as if we were looking at a landscape. We calmly observe these psychic arabesques from a detached viewpoint.

Piero Ferrucci, *What We May Be*

There is a part of each of us that watches. Freud calls it the observing ego; Vedanta philosophy calls it the witness; Buddhism calls it the watcher. Buddhism says that ultimately even the watcher needs to be let go of. Vedanta philosophy argues that there is one central, immovable something against which all consciousness has meaning. This consciousness is the self. It tells us that to identify with Atman, or self, is our goal and that to identify with other things is false identification, or identification with that which is not self. False identification can lead only to despair.

Identifying with the witness allows us to observe the self in action and gives us enough separation from the action self to see what is going on. It also keeps us from overidentifying or getting lost in the personality. When we do not feel overly identified, we have less to defend and protect and more willingness to let go and grow. Identifying with a higher self gives freedom to change.

The greater our identification with higher self, the less our need to identify with objects and experiences that can bring only limited pleasure. We know too well as a culture that we only create more hunger when we overidentify with material things, seeking meaning and soul that the things do not contain, or when we go outside of ourselves to fill our emptiness. We gobble experience as if enough of it can fill our empty bellies, only to find that we feel emptier than before. Mistakenly, we assume we chose the wrong experience, so we seek another experience to gobble, to swallow whole, to overeat. We feel slightly satisfied for a week or two, then we are empty again. So we go to the experience over and over again, still missing the enduring fact, it's a God-shaped emptiness we're trying to fill, and what is not of God, soul and self cannot fill a God-shaped hole inside.

In a culture that worships what is outside a person rather than what is inside, it is a tremendous act of daring to turn inward and toward soul for life's true meaning and joy. By identifying with the soul, we are keeping "our treasures in heaven," remembering that though we live in the world, we are not of it, that our true natures are soul, changeless and everlasting.

Identifying with soul does not mean that we cannot enjoy the good life. In fact, identifying with soul better enables us to more effectively choose and seek out those experiences that are gratifying, and makes us more dynamic and effective in all our life activities.

Keeping the soul as the center of our reality allows us to bring soulful energy into life and to have the air of someone who is centered and happy with themselves. This kind of person naturally attracts other people because centeredness and self-contentment are qualities that we all wish for. One doesn't need to change homes, partners or professions in order to shift the deep identification within. In fact, changing all of these things can postpone one's ability to begin to identify with soul because there will be too much life confusion for one to simply sit and be.

Identifying with the witness and observing self in action requires only a shift in awareness, a shift in emphasis. Any life changes that need to be made will happen naturally when one gets used to this shift in perception.

◊

You can observe a lot just by watching.

Yogi Berra

COMMITMENT

*The person who does not make a choice
makes a choice.*

Jewish proverb

All too often we believe that if we choose the right person, profession or town, we will be happy. While certainly wise choice is a factor, how well we take care of what we have is an essential part of how well we build our happiness. All relation-

Don't change horses midstream.

Abraham Lincoln

ships, careers and endeavors need to be nurtured and tended if they are to grow and become strong and thriving. It is our commitment to something or someone that pays dividends in the long run. We are often better off working with what we have and making it right for us, rather than spending time chasing rainbows.

Commitment is necessary for a relationship to deepen, whether it is with the self, another person or a life's work. Without commitment, we do not stay to work through the tough stuff. When things get painful or scary or confusing, we leave. Unfortunately, we leave with our confusion and our load of pain because it is only in working through the fear and hurt that clarity comes. This is one of the ways that soul awareness gets generated; at the center of the search is soul waiting to be seen.

❦

He became an infidel, hesitating between two mosques.

Turkish proverb

SURRENDER

The way to do is to be.

Tao Te Ching

The internal position of surrender is a recognition that we are not in control of each and every event or circumstance of our lives. It is a chosen sense of powerlessness that allows us to be take-charge people, but frees us from the illusion of control, and the need to manipulate events and people.

There is a vast difference between being a take-charge person and a controlling person. A take-charge person knows how to work with the natural flow of events and personalities to accomplish something. She can allow room for providence and individual creativity to play a role. The controlling person, on the other hand, operates through an inflexible structure, attempting to manipulate people and situations to conform to a concept of right, perfect or appropriate, in the process shutting down others' creative contributions. Surrender allows us to act in consort with our surroundings, to act or to be still as the situation requires. The act of surrender is an act of faith that strengthens our relationship with God.

The concept of surrender runs contrary to the Western mind. We have been taught to go after what we want aggressively, to make things happen. But surrender asks us to allow events to unfold at their own pace, to get out of our own way and to let go of our desire for control. Surrender is an act of trust in the universe, an acknowledgment that there are forces beyond our own will at work in our lives.

Don't push the river.

❦

Everything comes if a man will only wait.

Benjamin Disraeli

APPRECIATION

Normal day, let me be aware of the treasure you are. Let me learn from you, love you, savor you, bless you before you depart. Let me not pass you by in quest of some rare and perfect tomorrow. Let me hold you while I may for it will not always be so. One day I shall dig my nails into the earth, or bury my face in the pillow, or stretch myself taut, or raise my hands to the sky, and want, more than all the world, your return.

Mary Jean Irion

Appreciating what we value in our lives helps it to persist. When we acknowledge and build on the positive qualities of behavior, we reward that behavior and so tend to get more of it. So it is with all of our interactions and circumstances in life—appreciation reinforces what went well and encourages more of it.

It works also on a subtle level. The appreciation that we feel in our hearts is felt by others, and when others feel it from us, they feel safe and make their better side more available to us. Even plants are influenced, growing or dying according to the energy and attention of the gardener.

Appreciation can be an energy that is felt by all that is alive around us. It can put us into a positive alignment with the creative energies present in our day-to-day lives, helping us to actually see, identify and co-create what we wish to have more of in daily living.

❦

Affirmation of life is the spiritual art by which man ceases to live life unreflectively and begins to devote himself to his life with reverence in order to raise it to its true value. To affirm life is to deepen, to make more inward, and to exalt the will to live.

Albert Schweitzer

BREATH AWARENESS

"Watching over the breath" consists in letting the breath come and go as it wants, without forcing it or clutching at it. In due course its rhythm automatically slows down, and it flows in and out so smoothly. This is both a symbol of and a positive aid to letting one's whole life come and go without grasping.

Alan Watts, *Nature, Man and Woman*

Breath awareness is one of the key practices in soul awareness. Breath brings the soul into the body and brings the spirit into the material. Breath awareness is simple. Just sit quietly and become aware of your breathing a few minutes each day to train yourself to connect with breath. Breathe in and out easily and completely, without a pause between inhalation and exhalation, and relax. Allow the mind to clear. Observe how being aware of the breath affects your intunement with the moment.

You can do this anywhere, any time. When you become familiar with this process, carry it into daily living. Whether sitting, standing, walking or engaging in activities, become aware of your breath. Often you will find that you have been holding your breath. Relax and center yourself and bring yourself back into the moment. Breath draws soul into the moment and calms the nervous system. It is an invaluable tool for centering the self virtually any time.

🌿

There are a number of breathing techniques you can use to make life vivid and more enjoyable. The first exercise is very simple. As you breathe in, you say to yourself, "Breathing in, I know that I am breathing in." And as you breathe out, say, "Breathing out, I know that I am breathing out." Just that.

Thich Nhat Hanh, *Peace Is Every Step*

MEDITATION

What then should we "do" with the mind in meditation? Nothing at all.
Just leave it, simply, as it is.

Sogyal Rinpoche, *The Tibetan Book of Living and Dying*

Meditation is one of the surest and perhaps most dependable ways to move into soul awareness. Meditation became popular in the United States through the teachings of Transcendental Meditation, an easy technique adapted to busy Americans lives. Also, it allowed meditation to be used as a tool for life enhancement separate from the sense of religion or ritual that traditionally had surrounded it.

Meditation essentially is a dropping down into an awareness of what is. The regular practice of meditation has countless benefits. Among them are increased knowledge of self, stress reduction, calming of the autonomic nervous system, increased capacity for concentration and focused activity, as well as an increase in the ability to access soul awareness.

In the Eastern tradition, meditation follows one of two streams. The first is development of concentration by focusing the mind on something, the breath, a thought, a light or a mantra. The benefits are in increased power of mind and greater tranquility. The goal is to keep the mind focused and to reach greater levels of absorption in the object and one-pointedness of mind. The other stream is insight meditation, which develops a moment-to-moment awareness of what is happening in one's life process. The goal is to stay awake to and within each changing moment and to witness the very process of living. The benefits of this type of meditation are greater insight into self and soul and eventual spiritual transformation.

Meditating even a few minutes once or twice a day and slowly expanding your capacity for stillness will have countless benefits. The simple act of meditating will cut the chatter of mind and help it to still itself, allowing you to be more creative, spontaneous and present in the moment, present to the soul in the here and now. Meditation allows a relationship with the soul to deepen, creating connection with the deeper self and an increased awareness of its varieties of expression in day-to-day living. Meditation opens a channel between the inner and the outer self, which increases our capacity to live more fully in a state of soul awareness.

The technique of meditation is simple. The idea is to still your body, quiet your mind and follow your breath, or focus on an inner object such as a word, a sound or a mantra. The idea is to be present to what is happening in the here and now, to your internal process, but not to get caught up in it. First, find a comfortable position sitting, or if necessary, lying down. Next, quiet and regulate your breathing. When thoughts arise, do not hang onto them. Allow them to move through your mind and simply witness them with no thought of controlling or interfering with them or following them in any particular direction. A helpful image is to imagine that your stream of thought is a river, and you are sitting on the bank of the river watching the thoughts flow by, with no more thought to controlling them than you would imagine the river.

In meditation you observe attachments by which you have heretofore defined yourself. Meditation gives you the sense of being connected to the source of all life, the original parent of all that lives, God energy, soul energy. This provides a sense of fullness and wholeness that neither can be given nor taken away. It is a birthright. A sense of belongingness is a basic need for human growth and well-being. It is our sense of belonging to something greater than ourselves—soul or God energy—that helps to protect us against the fear of being accepted or rejected by others. We will always be anxious and try to please others if we need *their* acceptance in order to accept *ourselves*. In order to feel whole, we will be enslaved by the very people from whom we need approval. When we come to understand that the source of all that is, is the true identity of our divine parent in heaven, then we will come to rest contentedly in the living arms of soul.

۷

Rest in natural great peace.

Nyoshul Khenpo

BONDING WITH THE SOUL

APPRECIATION

Reflection: Allow yourself to sit or lie in a comfortable position. Allow yourself to count your blessings, enjoy seeing what is beautiful and good in your life as it passes before your inner vision. Feel deeply the richness of your life and let your heart be full.

Journal: One of the paths of spirituality is gratitude. Feeling gratitude and appreciation is a way of opening the door to what is good in life and allowing it to manifest. Make a "Gratitude List." Write down each and every person, place and thing—past and present—in your life that you are grateful for.

BONDING WITH THE SOUL

CREATIVE VISUALIZATION

Reflection: Visualize a circumstance or situation that you want in your life. See it. Feel it. Image yourself as you participate in this circumstance *as if it were actually happening.* Move through this circumstance, interacting with it and experiencing it in your mind as if it were real and in your life now.

Journal: Write a journal entry of just a few lines describing some aspect of this circumstance as if it were happening now. Just report it in your journal. For example, if the situation your are imaging is of a comfortable relationship, the entry might read, "Jay and I had a lovely day today. As we had nothing special to do, we spent the day walking and picnicking in the park. Had a fun time." Let the entry be brief and matter-of-fact. You can visualize it over and over.

BONDING WITH THE SOUL

BECOMING AWARE OF EMOTIONAL TRIGGERING

Reflection: Allow yourself to reflect on a situation that has happened in the past month in which you feel you overreacted. That is, that your reaction was larger than the situation merited. Imagine the situation just as it happened. Pay attention to the point at which you became overheated. When you get to that point, focus on the behavior or the circumstance that triggered your heated response.

Journal: In your journal, all over one page, put words and phrases that describe your feelings at the moment you felt triggered. Look over what you have written. Begin to free-associate.

- What comes to mind when you look at these words and phrases?

- What unspoken feelings or words, what unresolved pain from the past might be adding fuel to your present reaction?

- Separate and identify which situation from the past causes you to overreact in the present.

Though thou hast ever so many counselors,
yet do not forsake the counsel of your own soul.

John Ray

ABOUT THE AUTHOR

Tian Dayton, Ph.D. in clinical psychology and M.A. in educational psychology, is a therapist in New York City and director of Innerlook, Inc. She is a certified psychodramatist and faculty member at New York University, and is also an AMS-certified Montessori teacher and a consultant at ONSITE, Caron Foundation and the Institute for Sociotherapy.

Tian Dayton's work includes seminal development in the field of psychodrama, training for senior-level health professional, and workshop presentations both for the public and for the therapeutic community. She is the author of several books appropriate for the lay reader and for the healing professional.

If you would like your name to be put on a mailing list to obtain information about workshops on soul issues and/or psychodrama across the United States, please send your name address and phone number to:

> Tian Dayton, Ph.D.
> Innerlook, Inc.
> 262 Central Park West
> Suite 4A
> New York, NY 10024

Other HCI Books by Tian Dayton

The Drama Within
Psychodrama and Experiential Therapy
A comprehensive book on psychodrama. It brings together a complete explanation of the theory and practice of psychodrama, directions for specific drama games, and methods for applying theory and games in the treatment of trauma and addiction.
Code 2964 . . . . $14.95

Keeping Love Alive
Inspirations for Commitment
Ideas for appreciating differences, honoring uniqueness and allowing space between two people who love each other.
Code 2603 . . . . $ 7.95

Daily Affirmations for Forgiving and Moving On
Powerful Inspiration for Personal Change
This book offers positive affirmations of hope, strength and inspiration to free you from the past and help you move on with your life.
Code 2158 . . . . $ 7.95

Daily Affirmations for Parents
How to Nurture Your Children and Renew Yourself During the Ups and Downs of Parenthood
Learn how to renew yourself with positive thoughts and uplifting affirmations to get you through the trials and tribulations of parenthood.
Code 1518 . . . . $ 5.95

Drama Games
Techniques for Self-Development
This book contains almost 100 drama games that can be used to sharpen communication skills and enhance self-esteem, used as therapy for adults or used with students in the classroom.
Code 021X . . . . $ 7.95

For Visa or MasterCard orders call **1-800-441-5569**. Your response code is **HCI**. Prices do not include Shipping & Handling.

Give the Gift that Keeps on Giving:
CHICKEN SOUP FOR THE SOUL

Inspire the special people in your life with a copy of *Chicken Soup for the Soul* and *A 2nd Helping of Chicken Soup for the Soul.* Sometimes it's hard to find the perfect gift for a loved one, friend or coworker. Readers of all backgrounds have been inspired by these books; why not share the magic with others? Both books are available in paperback for $12.95 each and in hard cover for $24.00 each (plus shipping and handling). You're sure to enrich the lives of everyone around you with this affordable treasure. Stock up now for the holidays. Order your copies today!

Chicken Soup for the Soul (paperback)
Code 262X $12.95
Chicken Soup for the Soul (hard cover)
Code 2913 . . . . $24.00
A 2nd Helping of Chicken Soup for the Soul (paperback)
Code 3316 . . . . $12.95
A 2nd Helping Of Chicken Soup for the Soul (hard cover)
Code 3324 . . . . $24.00

Lift Your Spirits with *Chicken Soup for the Soul Audiotapes*

Here's your chance to enjoy some *Chicken Soup for the Soul* and the ears. Now you can listen to the most heartwarming, soul-inspiring stories you've ever heard in the comfort of your home or automobile, or anywhere else you have a tape player.

Two of America's most beloved inspirational speakers, Jack Canfield and Mark Victor Hansen use their consummate storytelling ability to bring to life their bestselling collection. You'll hear tales on loving yourself and others; on parenting, learning and acquiring wisdom; and on living your dream and overcoming obstacles.

Special Gift-Set Offer: All three volumes
(6 cassettes—7 hours of inspirations) for only $29.95 + S&H
(a 27% discount). *Best Value!*

Volume 1: On Love and Learning to Love Yourself
(2 60-minute cassettes) Code 3070 . . . . $12.95
Volume 2: On Parenting, Learning and Eclectic Wisdom
(2 60-minute cassettes) Code 3081 . . . . $12.95
Volume 3: On Living Your Dream and Overcoming Obstacles
(2 90 minute cassettes)
Code 309X $14.95

Mail in your order form or call 1-800-441-5569 for Visa or MasterCard orders. Prices do not include shipping and handling.
Your response code is HCI.

Your Soul Journey Begins Today

Recovery of the Sacred
Lessons in Soul Awareness
Carlos Warter, M.D., Ph.D.

Here is the book that everyone is talking about by the author who is quickly approaching the status of Marianne Williamson, Deepak Chopra and James Redfield. This may be the most fascinating story you will ever read: and it is all true. *Recovery of the Sacred* is the mesmerizing tale of Dr. Carlos Warter's spiritual journey down paths of which few even dream: Studying with Idries Shaw, Claudio Naranjo, Alain Naude, Frederick Leboyer and Lama Thartang Tulku Rimpoche. Learning rituals of Shamanism, spiritual traditions of Sufism, Christian, Jewish and Islamic mysticism, Buddhist techniques of meditation. Traveling from Chile to Mexico, Machu Picchu, the Rockies, Morocco and the Holy Land. Don't dare miss it!
Code 3138..**$9.95**

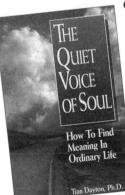

The Quiet Voice of Soul
How to Find Meaning in Ordinary Life
Tian Dayton, Ph.D.

This wonderful book illuminates for you the many ways in which soul can be seen and heard: through family, relationships, feelings, play, the universe and spirituality. Tian Dayton has written a work with the same power as *Care of the Soul*. An uplifting read that will inspire you.
Code 3391...**$9.95**

The Soul of Adulthood
Opening the Doors . . .
John C. Friel, Ph.D. and Linda Friel, M.A.

The Friels explain to you the connection between true adulthood and the deeper realms of your own soul in this transfixing book. Adulthood is a quality of soul that is chosen and earned through the deepening struggles that life offers as you progress from birth to death. A work that will open the doors to your soul.
Code 3413..**$9.95**

For Visa or MasterCard orders call: 1-800-441-5569 response code HCI. Prices do not include S&H.